Teach Your Dad
How to Fish

Teach Your Dad How to Fish

BY BURR SMIDT

Illustrations by the Author

Brooke House Publishers

CHATSWORTH, CALIFORNIA

Library of Congress Cataloging in Publication Data

Smidt, Burr, 1927-
    Teach your dad how to fish.

    1. Fishing. I. Title
SH441.S64   799.1   77-499
ISBN 0-912588-43-8

For my Dad, in memory.
    He untangled a lot of lines for me.

For my children, Jody, Amy, Nate and Mike,
    who tangled them up again.

And for my wife, Renee,
    who's tangled up my heart.

Love.

Contents

Color Illustrations

Acknowledgments

My thanks go to three people who contributed greatly to the conservation of trout this past fishing season:

My publisher, Mr. Louis Eaton, whose faith kept me desk-bound, constantly amazed, and dubiously happy at missing the best fishing season in living memory.

My editor, Mr. Jerome Fried, who should have an "n" before the "d" in his name. His vast knowledge and patience almost made up for lost fishing time.

Ms. Kadi Tint, our book designer, whose fastidious attention to detail kept most of my thumbprints off the artwork.

Teach Your Dad
How to Fish

Introduction

SOME STRAIGHT TALK

With the aid of this book, you are going to be a teacher. A teacher of fact and in fact a teacher of fishing.

Right here, up front, let me begin by making you a promise. There will be no cut-and-dried teaching of subjects like *reading* or *math* or *language* or *art* or *religion* . . . at least *not like you've known teaching.*

There will be reading, for sure, like: How to *READ* water. The math will be simple, just inches and pounds. And the language, a fisherman's language, excited and sweet: "I've got another one, Dad! He jumps like a Rainbow!" The art that you teach will be the color of life seen beyond limits (denied to those who don't fish) and the religion is one that needs no defining, for it's as open as love of the world and her creatures and as simple as peace.

Your pupil will be one it'll be fun to teach. He's taught *you* a lot; now you'll turn the tables and teach him, your Dad, something *you* know. And, by the time you've learned what this book and some real fishing have to teach *you,* you'll know a great deal that your Dad will be most interested in.

You may think that all of this is a large order for a young teacher to handle; well, perhaps—but you'll find that it all goes together and it fits to make a whole and that is part of and the best of my promise.

About this business of teaching

First, make a note to yourself to be patient with Dad. You must be prepared to explain everything in depth and detail and to show him. That is the way that he'll learn. You will be assigning Dad a workload of practice and study that you as his teacher feel he can comfortably handle. Remember, some dads can handle more of a workload than others; determine your own Dad's capacity and then keep him at it. Still on this thought, let me point out that you as the teacher are in a far better position to know your pupil than I . . . but I can loosely lump fathers together for you and hope with the *lumping* to touch on a point or two that you may have overlooked in your own evaluations of Dad. Every point we make, every trait we uncover, will give *you* as a teacher more productive methods of teaching.

GENERAL LOOSE LUMPING TOGETHER OF DADS:

1. Be it known that all dads were once young boys. Young boys more often than not love to fish. Therefore, presume that somewhere there is still a strong pattern working. Play that up, and your percentage of success should be quite high.

2. Most dads are very warm and enjoy doing things with you. (And if I must say so myself, fishing's the best thing.)

3. Generally, fathers like to set good examples, particularly as regards any kind of study (Dad wants to make a better person out of you). Play this up for all it's worth . . . and both of you study. It will make better persons out of *both* of you.

4. Fathers are generally very competitive. Now, in fact, fishing is not really a competitive sport, but chances are that Dad will try to make it one. Good! It's an easy trait to work on, because after you have outfished him a few times he will *really* get into the learning habit.

5. Fathers are basically reactive (somewhat like putty). They respond readily to subtle pressures—in this case pleasant stimuli: waterfalls, babbling brooks, the smell of fresh pine, warm beaches and boats, evenings beneath brilliant stars . . . comradeship, love, and pride. Of course, you won't have to teach him any of these things, they are all quite instinctive. You, as a teacher, just reinforce and remind.

I should think that it makes sense at this point to think about fish for a moment. You might as well know that, though this book will help you teach Dad a great deal about fishing and fish, neither this book nor any other can do more than scratch the surface of knowledge of fish. The subject is simply too vast to cram into even a lifetime of study.

There are over 20,000 species of fish. New ones are recognized and added to the list every year. There is no more diversified grouping of living things on, in, or over this earth, as regards size, habit, and distribution. Fish range from the tiniest and most delicate of forms to giants like the Basking and Whale Sharks that weigh many tons and grow fifty feet long. There are Arctic forms and Tropical forms—there are forms found in the mountains at high altitudes—forms in the depths of the oceans (too deep for our true understanding); there are fish that climb trees and walk across land—fish that are faster than birds or the cheetah or so slow that we must measure their progress in inches per hour; there are fish that live lifetimes (longer than man's) but never move far from their homes in reefs close to shore, while others roam thousands of miles across oceans each year. Fish live in a wide range of waters from salt to fresh . . . and every conceivable taste in between. There are fish that change sex from female to male and then back again, or perhaps not, but they could . . . it gets quite confusing. There are fish that lay eggs and others that give living birth; there are fish without scales, others with armor, some flat as a pancake or shaped like a snake, some with tails like a whip or a snout like a sword, some with fierce teeth while others sprout barbels like whiskers; some that suck up their food (like you eat spaghetti) and some that light up the entrance to their jaws for curious littler fish to investigate. And there are fish we call living fossils, almost unchanged from their ancestors who lived millions of years ago—hundreds of millions of years before even the great dinosaurs. So, you see, it's a mighty big order to lay onto Dad all at once.

Let's play it cool. Ease him into it by concentrating on only those fish that you and your Dad are most likely to catch. But be happy to know that they are the cream of the crop, the *game fish* most frequently sought after.

Let's introduce them to Dad and explain that one or a number of these species can be caught almost any place in the world (sometimes under names different from the ones we generally know them by). If Dad should insist that one of the fish listed in this book is found in the Indian Ocean—and that a trip to the Indian Ocean is out—just smile and explain that any fish listed here that might be found in the Indian Ocean—or wherever—will also be found (somewhat surprisingly) close to you here at home. The oceans are all one and there are no land barriers between them as there are water barriers between continents.

The fishes of our book will be listed as either *freshwater* or *saltwater* species. There are a few that are found in both tastes of water. When you have studied more about these you will explain them—the how and the why—to your Dad.

THE FISHES OF OUR BOOK

In freshwater:

Bass, Trout, and Salmon (and their relatives). The Pike (and his relatives).

In saltwater:

Bluefish, Striped Bass, Weakfish (and relatives), Mackerel (and relatives), Snook, Bonefish, Tarpon, the Tuna, Dolphin, and Billfish.

In addition to the sport fishes listed above, we will come to know and to love a group from both freshwater and saltwater that I call "just plain old *fun fishes.*" You can explain to Dad that there are times of the year when certain game fishes are by nature or law out of season. This is part of the fun in studying: to know who is out traveling and where, and the why, and, of course, when they'll be home. At times of the year when the others are gone or taboo, the fun fish take over to sharpen our skills. And for goodness sakes don't ever look down your nose at them, the Crappies and Bluegills, the Jacks and the Groupers and Snappers, for you'll find that pound for pound many of our fun fish can fight harder than their more celebrated and sportier cousins.

At this point, I think it only fair to warn you that either you or your Dad will hook and land somebody that is not covered here in the book. It is hoped that with study you will be able to work out for yourselves—if not his name—at least a good guess as to the family of fishes he belongs to. Another thing that you as the teacher should know right away as you work with this book is "the subject of *bait.*" Its not in the book, at least not in the true sense of the word, for here we will stress fishing only with *lures,* artificials you've made or those that have proven good and that you've bought. Now, I'm not against fishing with worms or other kinds of bait. Not at all. I just think that *lures are more fun.* You can explain some of the reasons why this is undoubtedly so. I'll list some reasons and later you'll add a few of your own.

REASONS FOR LURES BEING BETTER THAN BAIT:

1. You want to match wits with the fish—to arrive at a point of true understanding.

2. You want Dad to be selective in the fish that he takes (remember we are after the cream of the crop).

3. You want Dad to be fair—to think of the fish (with a lure they seldom "swallow" the hook). With your help he will catch quite a few and *release* quite a few. Keep only those that you want for your dinner.

4. Part of the fun when fishing with lures is the tackle, the making and tying of flies, the thoughts that go with the feathers, the fur, and the tinsel. (With the help of this book you can show your Dad how.)

5. (*Important*) It should be almost no time at all before you have Dad to the point where he can outfish any bait fisherman alive; it takes knowledge and time but he'll do it.

6. Fish that you take with a lure hit with a flash and fight harder.

7. (*Note*) Also, a great many fishermen-fathers like the fact that without worms they can travel *cleaner* and further.

8. The skill of the fly, unlike the luck of the bait, is a magnet that will pull both you and your Dad out into the world seeking thrills and adventure—that's what sport's all about.

When you think about it, the fish that you take with artificials are generally referred to as *game fish.* I hope that tells you something *up front.* Also, I think that your Dad will like the mobility that fishing with artificials affords. He'll find himself moving about, "working" the stream (perhaps walking for miles—it's good exercise), walking, working, and casting the shores of a lake, casting, constantly casting (except when he's tied to a fish at the other end of the line), or out on the sea in a boat, moving along with the fish. It is far more interesting than being anchored to just one special spot. He will soon get to know the area well, quickly find out where the fish are. Now, if Dad doesn't buy this concept of moving about . . . well, then, just let him sit. He'll follow your lead soon enough if you practice it and you are the one who shows up with dinner.

Now that we have released all our worms and decided that we are going to get Dad into the delightful business of tricking his fish, let us start by convincing him that fish of either freshwater or saltwater readily take artificials. The problem is simply picking the lures that the fish want. We'll narrow these lures down to a few that I know will take fish any place at all in the world. I don't mean that you should not experiment; by all means you should, either with ones that you've made or the ones that some manufacturer claims are the best (at some times and in some places they are), but be assured that if you carry the ones that are recommended here in the book you'll almost always take fish.

Now: Let's put a fish in your place for a moment (that's a switch). He sits at the table where you sit when you're hungry. (Isn't it amazing? You always seem to know where to go when you're hungry.) So, let's give him a choice as he sits at your place. A tasty looking "Big Burger," side order of fries, and a shake; or a steaming bowl of yesterday's farina and a glass of warm buttermilk. He pauses a minute (as you would), then hungrily reaches for (who wouldn't?) the burger. Ah! But he's fooled; it was all made of plastic and sponge . . . and even you (smart as you are, knowing it's a fake) would have taken it first, because you are *curious* or maybe just *mad* that you had been fooled.

Fish, in or out of your place, are like that. Did you ever wonder (if you even up till now had thought of it) why fish or game fish are so nimble and quick? Well, it's because they have to chase and run down their food, which is also nimble and quick. You certainly wouldn't let a Hershey bar get away from you just because it could run, but chances are that you'd be chasing the wrapper, because that is what you'd recognize: a delicious brown paper wrapper with **great silver letters (that spell HERSHEY).** I bet you'd be in a fighting mad mood if, when you caught it, you found that the inside was made of wood. Explain to Dad that artificials should look and act the way that fish think that they should. Let him in on all of your secrets, such as speed of retrieve or action imparted and depth to be fished (as we continue this primer for teachers we'll learn all of these things).

HINTS AND CLUES:

Keep your eyes peeled for hints and suggestions. It might even help Dad if you were to *underline* clues that you find in the text and the stories.

For example, the type and the shape of a fish's fins—most particularly his *caudal* fin (the correct name for his tail)—can help you and your Dad identify at least the family that the fish you caught might belong to. Knowing this one thing alone might easily increase your "luck" for the day a hundredfold. I'll cite an example of just how it might. You and your Dad are out in a boat with other fishermen and someone catches a fish. You look at the fish, and none of you knows who he is. Let's now assume that Dad does not know a thing about tails (which probably means he does not know a thing about fish). You, on the other hand, do. Dad says, "Gee, he's pretty. Let's catch another one," and proceeds to drop his lure to the bottom. "That's where the big ones are!" he says.

But smart little you size up the tail and you say, "It's *lunate,* and look at the finlets!"

"How's that again?" says your Dad.

"I mean," you say, "that it's crescent-shaped. *That* fish belongs to the Mackerel family!" Then you go on to explain (if you want your Dad to keep up with you as you start catching fish) that these are fish that travel and feed near the surface. Most "Mackerel" prefer something that's light or flashy in lures, which, as you know, must be worked and retrieved rather fast. It might help if you start to troll and try to locate the school (almost all of the Mackerel family travel in rather large schools).

On the other hand, let's suppose that the fish that was caught had a square tail. You might have observed that this one is TRUNCATE (shaped like a broom). The chances are that this guy, if he has a dark color and a big mouth, is a Grouper because he lives near the bottom, and you know what kind of a bottom he likes—wrecks or rocks, underwater obstructions, coral and caves.

You see! Not only have you pinpointed his family, but you know something about what the bottom is like. You might even hope that you'll take a **Snapper** or two since a number of that family like the same kind of spots.

When you feel that he's ready and has learned well what you've taught, run a quiz. A good time to do this is on the way to your first fishing trip. Make him point out when you've arrived at the lake, stream or the shore, the places and spots that he thinks are most likely to be productive of fish. Ask him what kind, what lure he suggests, what time of day he thinks best. Humor him when you think that he's wrong and by all means laugh at his jokes. Keep him optimistic at all times—talk a lot about whales (that you know he won't catch). Believe me he'll be happy with a Trout or a Bass . . . and again I remind you "be patient". If he doesn't look like an expert on the very first day . . . if you've handled your end of the teaching . . . at least he's well on his way.

A clue to remember: Study the pictures and maps that I've devoted to you, use them as guides to knowing your fish and the waters. It's really quite easy. Fish, like almost all wild creatures, are creatures of habit. They follow interesting patterns of movement and feeding in their watery home; the conditions that have shaped these patterns are generally typical from stream to stream, lake to lake, or along any stretch of the shore.

If you study the anatomy drawings on the opposite page, it'll all come together.

Anatomy of a typical modern fish

1st dorsal fin (spiny)

2nd dorsal fin (soft rays)

caudal peduncle

nares

lateral line

cheek

mandible

gill opening

pectoral fin (paired)

pelvic fin (paired)

anal fin

Homocercal "type" caudal fin (tail) typical of Bass, Sunfish

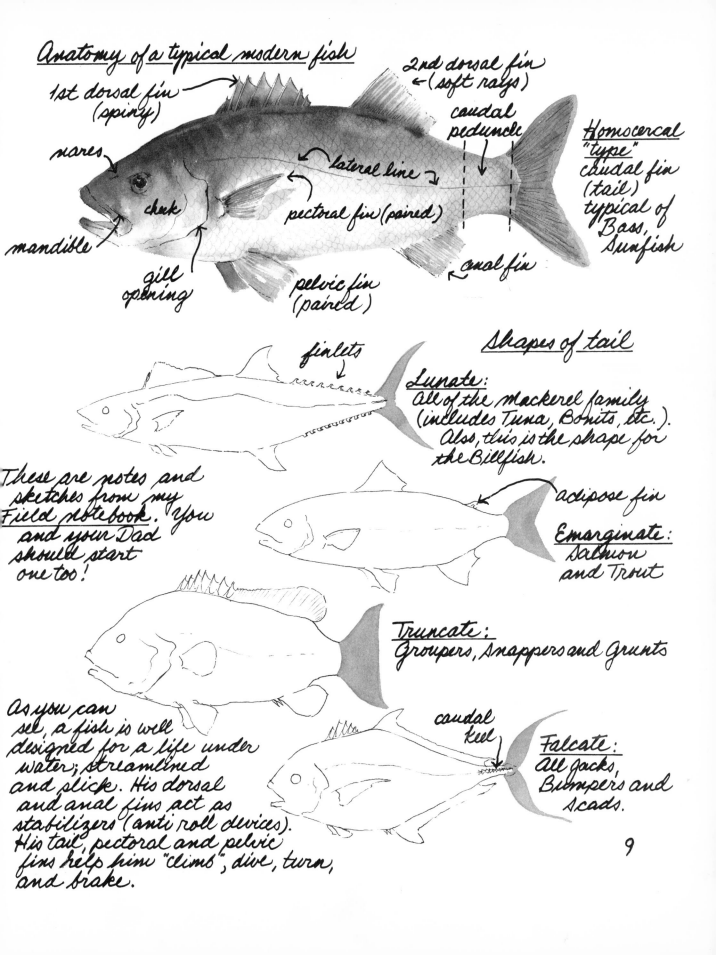

Shapes of tail

finlets

Lunate: All of the mackerel family (includes Tuna, Bonito, etc.). Also, this is the shape for the Billfish.

These are notes and sketches from my Field notebook. You and your Dad should start one too!

adipose fin

Emarginate: Salmon and Trout

Truncate: Groupers, Snappers and Grunts

As you can see, a fish is well designed for a life under water; streamlined and slick. His dorsal and anal fins act as stabilizers (anti roll devices). His tail, pectoral and pelvic fins help him "climb", dive, turn, and brake.

caudal keel

Falcate: All Jacks, Bumpers and Scads.

9

most common types of dorsal fins

single usually soft rays

(Bonefish, Ladyfish, Herring! Minnows)

1st dorsal (spiny) — separated → 2nd dorsal (soft)

(Striped Bass, Weakfish, Barracudas)

1st — joined → 2nd

(Sunfish, Bass, Groupers, Snappers, Perch, etc.)

1st — 2nd — 3rd

(Cods, Pollock, Haddock)

A few oddly shaped fish and fin arrangements

the "Look Down" (Selene Drewoortii)

His *tail* shape suggests that he is related to the Jacks.

more primitive types of tails

Heterocercal (Sharks)

Diphycereal (Lampreys and Ratfish)

Pointed (Eels)

This is a living fossil, the Coelacanth, thought to have been extinct for 60,000,000 years. Now caught off S. Africa.

Ocean Sunfish (Mola, Mola) One of the head fishes. Reported to reach over 2,000 pounds. (They are harmless and beautiful)

Queen Triggerfish (Balistes Vetula) common in the Carribean)

10

Among the notes and sketches in the back of the book are some dealing with *tackle*. Use these to help Dad understand about the tools that he'll use. (I'm sure that YOU already know a great deal about it.)

Also, if I happen to mention a fish in an offhand way, and he's somebody that you don't know very well, look him up in the index that begins on page 219. (You'll be surprised to find that, perhaps by the time you finish the book, he'll be a good friend.)

The book is divided in the following way (to make it easy for you as a teacher).

Part I deals with FRESHWATER FISHING AND FISH.

Part II takes you down to the sea for SALTWATER FISH (where you'll meet both monsters and sweethearts).

After each chapter on a particular fish, I will tell you a story about something that happened to me. (Most of the stories are loaded with clues for you.) As a matter of fact, I think I'll start off with a story, one about the Black Bass (who is one of the "Who's Who" of freshwater fish).

Part One
•
Freshwater Fishing & Fish

I believe that I might just have been able to teach *my* Dad something about how to catch Bass. It all took place when I was young. I guess that's a nice thing about fishing and maybe about Bass in particular; you seem able to magically remember everything.

I lived on the beach on the Gulf Coast of Florida, a totally enjoyable place at a totally enjoyable time. I was eight when this took place, so it was a long time ago. If there had been any fault in my education up to that time, it was that my fishing experience had been limited to saltwater, which was perfectly natural since it was only a few yards away. My only problem was finding and procuring bait.

You see, in those days I knew about bait only and I prided myself on the fact that I caught all my own. Sometimes, and for some fish, I was happy with *fiddlers,* small colorful crabs that swarmed near their burrows on a tidewater flat close to home. If you didn't mind getting nipped a little bit once in a while, they were easy to catch: just scoop them up and plunk them down in a pail. They are a wonderful bait for any number of saltwater fish, most particularly for Sheepshead, a kind of overgrown Porgy, with stripes. Fiddlers were also good bait for a fish that I will tell you about in the chapter on saltwater fun fish (page 175), the Redfish or Channel Bass, sometimes known by the name of Red Drum. I confess that at that time I had never managed to catch a Redfish (at least I confess to that now). He was simply too big and too strong for the tackle I used, which consisted of any old string and/or wire that I found around home. The rod, or rather the pole, that I used was fresh-cut green bamboo, right from the yard. I say fresh-cut because the bamboo would dry up and shrivel in a matter of days; it had to be replaced as it lost all its bounce and its spring . . . which I guess didn't matter when it came to the Redfish anyway. For though I hooked quite a few, it was always with the same sad result: the Redfish would head out for the middle of the bay as fast or as slow as it pleased, completely unmindful of me. My line, my bamboo, my arms, would straighten right out and go pop! Well, not truly my arms, which would always recover after they had shaken a bit.

As everyone knows, one thing tends to lead to the next and so it is with this story. I was out scouting for bait. There was a creek near my home that ran to the bay. I had absolutely no idea where it ran from. I had a vague idea that it flowed from a land made of mangroves, inhabited by pirates or cannibals—or both—which thought until now had kept me from going to look. To me that creek was as big as the Nile or the Amazon and twice as mysterious, which, when one thinks about it, was quite natural because I had not yet seen the Nile or the wide Amazon. To sweeten the story, I'll inform you that I was uncommonly brave in those days and that I was learning a great deal about myself; it had come more like a splash than a ripple when I realized that something inside of me would never let any uncharted body of water I faced go without challenge. So I summoned up courage.

It took me only a week once I decided to go, to go up that river with my tackle, my rod, and my pail full of fiddlers. I waded the river, enchanted by a blue heron who waded slowly a few yards up ahead. It seemed to me he was leading me on, and I silently hoped he's stay with me, for he seemed very courageous. I felt safe in his company. But wonders quickly unfolded. I was amazed and delighted at the new bait sources I found. For here, less than half a mile up the river, were rich oyster beds, the flat tide banks of the shore were alive with colorful armies of fiddlers and blue claw crabs scuttled away in front of my feet. There were literally schools of Mummichog Minnows, so I forgot about cannibals and pirates.

But one thing puzzled me greatly and that was the change in the water: its color. From the familiar seawater green it turned amber and, after another half mile, brown. I also noticed that it tasted less salty and that the plant growth along shore—where the river ran brown—was ever so strange. I really suppose that I knew about water lilies and hyacinth, though I had never seen them grow wild.

I stopped and sat on the shore marveling at all my discoveries and trying to put it all together as any decent explorer would. Point *one:* I reasoned (without any help) that my river of salt had turned into fresh water. Later I learned about brackish water, a mixture of waters, both fresh and salt. Another thing, and point *two:* many of the life forms and the fishes that I knew from the sea seemed equally at home here up the river. There were Mullet, and I spied a Sheepshead or two, as well as some wily gray Snappers and blue crabs swimming in either direction. It was a lot to digest for an eight-year-old, but I guess that's true of nearly everything in the way of the knowledge that you happen to stumble onto: that is what makes it so fresh and exciting. Anyway, I just sat and I thought as I twiddled an old piece of pine branch the size and the color of a half-smoked cigar. Absently I peeled off the bark and, when I was through with that small operation, I gave my cigar piece of wood a good heave, straight at a lily pad that I hoped to hit true. I was almost on mark. The water exploded right where it hit, and I experienced a quick rush of fright when the wooden cigar I had thrown went flying a couple of feet into the air. It was a long minute or two until the water settled back into calm and I realized that it had been a rather large fish. I had no idea what kind, but I began to fish with my fiddlers. I fished for all I was worth, but with no luck, except for a small Pinfish or two, and they hardly counted at all. Knowing that something important was swimming below, after an hour I decided that whoever he was, in the river was some strange wood-eating fish.

A courageous Blue Heron leads me up the "Pirate" river.

Even I, at that age, felt silly thinking that a fish would eat wood . . . but it gave me an idea. I remembered that in the small green metal tackle box that I carried was some sort of lure made of wood, one I had found weeks ago washed up on shore. I had laughed at it then, mainly because its hooks were practically rusted away and one of the small propellers at one end was busted in two. It had also been tangled in heavy black line, and when I found it I simply looked at it as some very bad fisherman's folly.

FRESHWATER
16 ● FISH

But now I straightened out that lure as best I could, tied it to the end of my line, swung it out, and plopped it down next to the lily pad I had used as a target.

There was an immediate swirl beneath the plug and once again the water exploded, and this time he jumped. He was a beautiful fish, all dark green, bronze, and black. He jumped only once . . . and then he dove for the bottom and even quicker than my old friend the Redfish he straightened my line, my pole, and my arms, and he was gone. When I got home (a little too late) I told my Dad about the wood-eating fish that I'd found. He smiled then and told me that he "guessed that it was time that I showed him how to catch fish." Later that week he bought me my first rod and reel and he seemed quite as surprised as was I at the variety and number of plugs made of wood, designed, no doubt, for my wood-eating fish. I can truthfully say that it was no time at all before I had my Dad up the river to my own secret place and catching those wonderful Bass, for that's what they were.

You can see how well I remember. I suppose it's because of a number of things, like the color of water or the cannibals or the schools of Mummichog Minnows or the brave wading birds in feathers of blue. But most of all I guess it was all of the fun in teaching my Dad how to fish for Black Bass.

Bass

One of America's most important freshwater fish is the Black Bass (*Micropterus*, his Latin scientific name is fun to know too): "Hey Dad! I see you caught a small-finned Micropterus." Actually BLACK BASS is a collective name that includes any of ten species of warm-water fish of the Sunfish family. They are fairly large and strong and readily take lures. The two principal fish of this species are the LARGEMOUTH and SMALLMOUTH BLACK BASS. They are very adaptable (live in many places and under many conditions). They are found in every state in the Union, with the possible exception of Alaska (poor Alaska!). Bigmouth and Smallmouth overlap each other's range in many parts of the country, but as a general rule try to think of Mr. Smallmouth as a Northerner and big ol' Mr. Largemouth as a Southerner. Both are fished in the same general manner, with the same type of tackle and lures.

Now, before we get down to the business of prying into Mr. Bass's affairs, let me mention in passing a few of the other species and subspecies of Black Bass. They have colorful names, but they are less important to us at this time because most of them have limited ranges. ("Range" in this sense simply means the area in which the species lives.) The NEOSHO SMALLMOUTH is a subspecies of the Northern Smallmouth. As might be expected he is found in the Neosho River of Kansas. His other favorite states are Kansas' neighbors, Oklahoma, Missouri, and Arkansas. The REDEYE BASS is found in Alabama, Georgia, and parts of Florida and Tennessee. Look for him in small streams. The SPOTTED BASS is a hybrid form,

Just for you, I've drawn some pictures of Bass on page 23.

probably a cross between the LARGEMOUTH and SMALLMOUTH. He is found from the Gulf states north to Ohio and into parts of the Midwest. The SUWANEE BASS, a small bass that seldom reaches a pound, comes from the river in Florida that gives him his name. What a beautiful home! FLORIDA LARGEMOUTH BASS, a subspecies of Largemouth, is found throughout Florida. He grows *very* large; a sixteen-pounder would not be uncommon. He has been transplanted to a number of lakes in Southern California (and like myself, also transplanted out "there," I'm sure he still thinks of himself as a Floridian). GUADALUPE BASS, unlike most things in Texas (his home), tends to be rather small. ALABAMA SPOTTED BASS is found in Alabama, Mississippi, and Georgia. WICHITA SPOTTED BASS lives in Oklahoma. (If I had been in charge of names, I would have named him after a town in Oklahoma rather than Wichita, which everyone knows is a city in Kansas.)

Tell Dad that if there are gangsters and mobs in the freshwater world undoubtedly they are all of these Bass. They are bullies and fighters and often strike out just because they are mad. They are sneaky and devious, more active at evening and night. They'll take almost anything that they can get into their oversized mouths, anything that wiggles or crawls or swims or lights on the water. Their diet includes other fish—even other bass that are almost their size—frogs and mice, small ducklings (with or without applesauce), worms, snakes, small turtles and, in fact, if they got any larger and if I was an alligator sharing their pond, I'd be pretty darned careful when swimming about.

It is easy to see that, with such a diet, there exists a wide range of lures designed to take Bass. Top-water *plugs* and/or *poppers, streamers* and *flies,* deep-running *plugs* and/or *jigs* and flashing *spinners,* not to mention *plastic worms* (which I don't understand but which they love).

Although I've branded the Bass the criminal class, don't let that unsettle you or scare you. Just change to a Superman outfit (waders and vest) and take Dad out to catch them.

Getting Down to Techniques:

The one thing about Bass that you must explain to your Dad is that because they are found under so many different conditions and types of water, we must employ our good common sense, that is, approach each situation with the attitude that best fits. As we get to know Bass, common sense will become second nature. Let's look at the "Bass" lake that is somewhere close by to you. If it is a shallow lake, with a wealth of old tree stumps that seem to sprout from the water, well, then, our common sense tells us that this is a lake that calls for surface types or shallow-running lures, poppers, and flies, of course. Any old lake has deep spots and a few holes (that is unless it's been lined with concrete, and then common sense would call it a pool in someone's backyard). Look for these spots, for Bass, like most fish, will head for the holes; this is particularly true during the heat of the day. At morning and dusk they move through the shallows, the weeds, and the brush, and these times of the day are the best times to fish along shore. I think that evenings are best, if for no other reason than that the day starts to cool and the winds almost always die down. There's a hush in the air and a strange sensation as instincts beyond your control go to work; you can feel, and you *know* that big fish are moving about. Let Dad in on that feeling and secret.

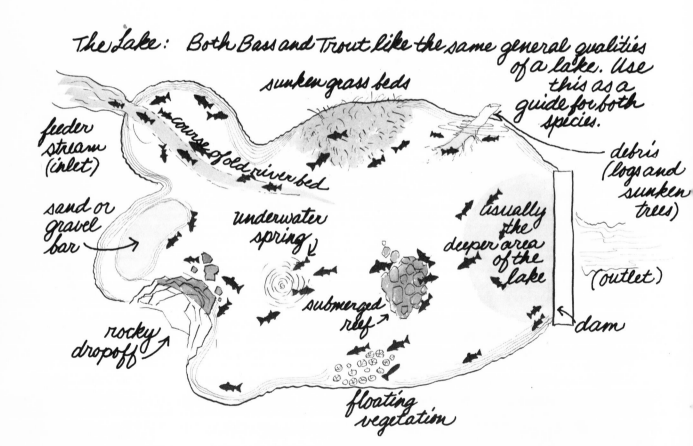

The Lake: Both Bass and Trout like the same general qualities of a lake. Use this as a guide for both species.

sunken grass beds

feeder stream (inlet)

course of old river bed

sand or gravel bar

debris (logs and sunken trees)

underwater spring

usually the deeper area of the lake

(outlet)

submerged reef

dam

rocky dropoff

floating vegetation

Fish near the stumps that are showing and, if you know where they are, by the ones that are not. It pays to do research; talk to Old Timers who grew up with the lake. (You'll meet the Old Timers at the tackle store—or out fishing. After you've talked to a few you'll know how to spot them by the gleam in their eyes.) Now, if your lake is large, generally deep, the type with a dam (a reservoir), you'll have to go deep with your lures. This is where lead-head jigs, deep-running plugs, and plastic worms go to work. Work your lures deep in the dropoffs near shore, find gravel bottom and bump your lure there (reasonably slow). Also look for rock ledges or bars and points that extend out from the shore. When you hook up, in deep water, you won't see all the action until he comes to the surface, but you'll feel it and feel sightly awed, for the fish that you take in these deep waters are as a rule somewhat larger than those of the shallower lakes—unless you live in a state like Florida (which is heaven for Bass and where almost all lakes are shallow).

If you knew Mr. Bass on a personal level, he would tell you that he is most comfortable when the water temperature is 65 to 70 degrees Fahrenheit. Bass spawn in the spring, when the water has reached this, their comfortable temperature range. It is at this time of the year that they seem most active and aggressive, providing the best of Bass fishing. Even in deep lakes you will have surface action at this time of the year. A clue to let Dad in on is that Bass are something of a schooling fish; they like to hang out together. Tell Dad that if he catches one fish he's likely to get more in the area.

Bass are also found in rivers and streams. The Largemouth seems to prefer the deeper, more sluggish sections, while the scrappy Smallmouth loves riffles and a rather fast flow. Smallmouth are indeed found in marginal areas that also hold Trout. You are liable to catch one or the other if you are lucky enough to find a condition like that (if you live in New England, your chances are better).

If you're lucky, you might have an opportunity to observe Bass in a clear-water lake. You might notice that they stalk their prey much in the manner of your pet tabby cat after a bird, and because of this feline trait they can often be teased into striking a lure. A twitch or a jiggle is often enough to bring them our charging like a reddogging football tackle. Tell Dad to try to play with them this way . . . fish them slowly . . . then give a tease and a twitch and hold on. It is a particularly effective technique when fishing the surface with floaters and poppers (also with slow crawling plastic worms on the bottom).

It is best to fish Bass from a boat, but it is also fun when it is done from the shore. The reason that a boat is best, however, is that many Bass lakes have overgrown shores with lily pads in a marsh round the edge. A rental rowboat will do nicely in most Bassy places. Believe it or not, there are also boats designed and equipped just for the fishing of Bass, flat-bottomed and fast, with a separate little motor running off a battery that is used to maneuver, steered by the feet to get you in close, with a whisper, to tangles and snags. When you see one of these boats with a Bass fisherman working, and you're hooked on this kind of work too, then get to work working on work that will buy one of these boats just for you.

How to Tell the Black Bass Apart

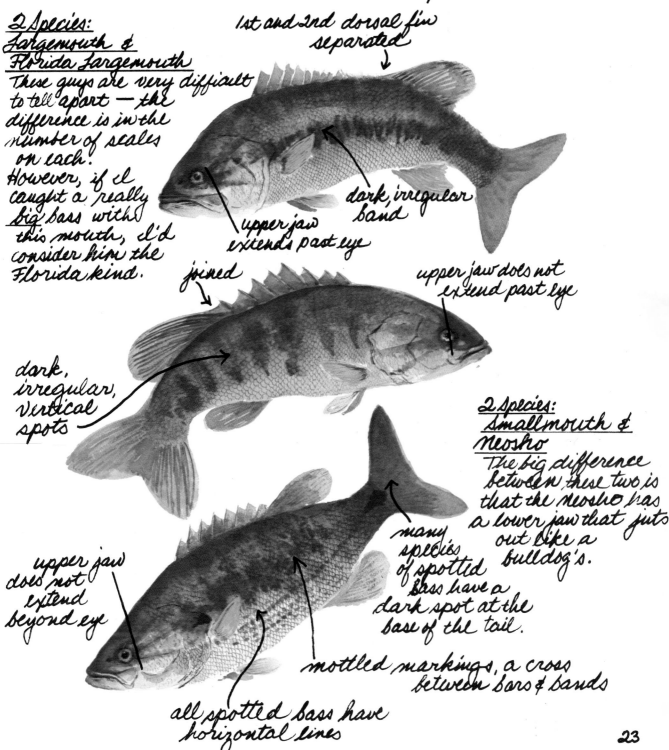

2 Species:
Largemouth &
Florida Largemouth
These guys are very difficult to tell apart — the difference is in the number of scales on each.
However, if I caught a really big bass with this mouth, I'd consider him the Florida kind.

1st and 2nd dorsal fin separated

dark, irregular band

upper jaw extends past eye

joined

upper jaw does not extend past eye

dark, irregular, vertical spots

2 species:
Smallmouth &
Neosho
The big difference between these two is that the Neosho has a lower jaw that juts out like a bulldog's.

upper jaw does not extend beyond eye

many species of spotted bass have a dark spot at the base of the tail.

mottled markings, a cross between bars & bands

all spotted bass have horizontal lines

23

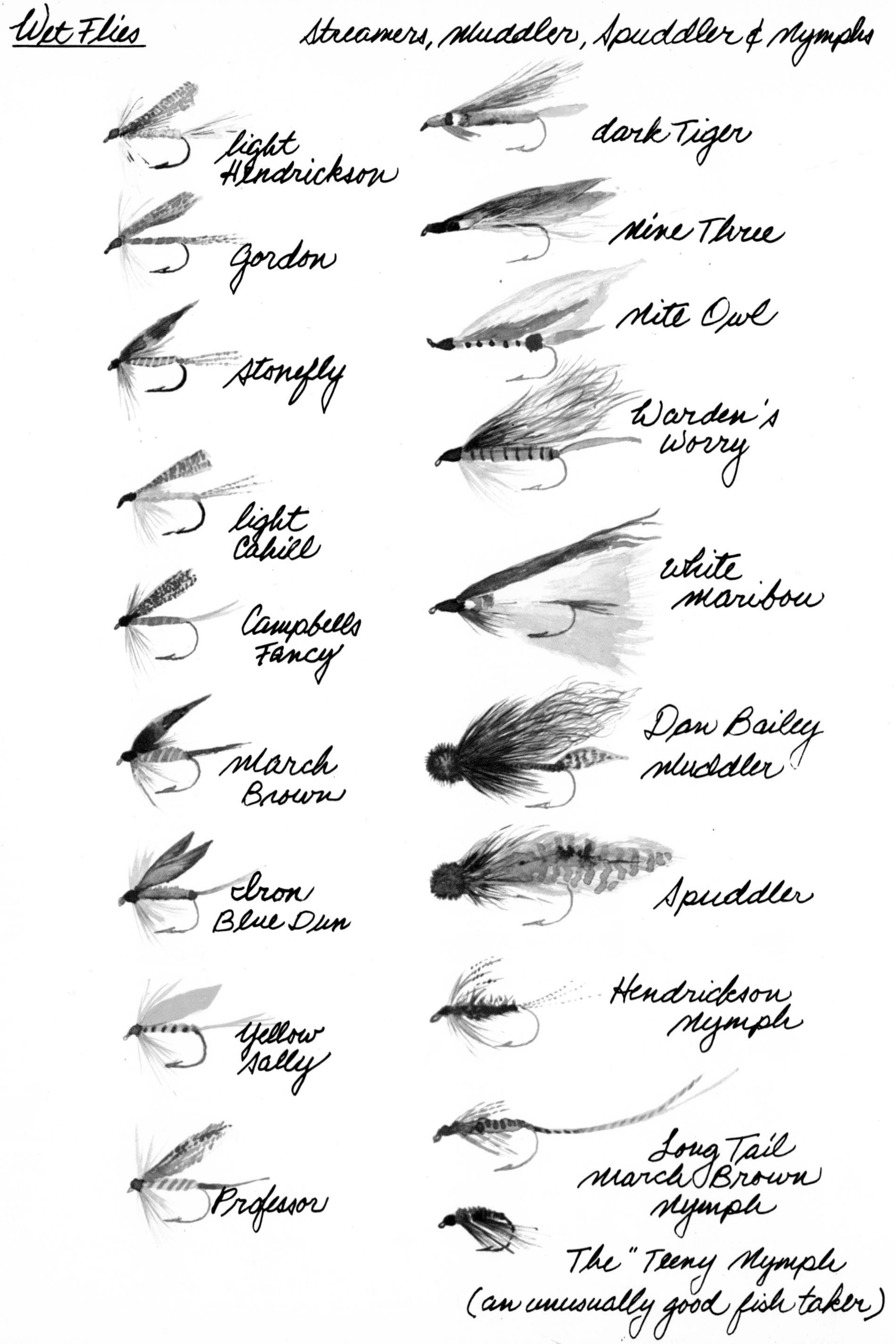

Wet Flies

Streamers, Muddler, Spuddler & Nymphs

light Hendrickson

Gordon

Stonefly

light Cahill

Campbells Fancy

March Brown

Iron Blue Dun

Yellow Sally

Professor

dark Tiger

nine Three

nite Owl

Warden's Worry

white maribou

Dan Bailey muddler

Spuddler

Hendrickson Nymph

Long Tail March Brown Nymph

The "Teeny Nymph (an unusually good fish taker)

Irresistible

Mosquito

Iron Blue Dun

White Wulff

Royal Coachman (Hairwing)

Brown Bivisible

Royal Coachman (Fanwing)

Athertherton 6

Grey Wulff

Black Gnat

Adams

Light Cahill

These few patterns should start your Dad off with the right bug!

A few Trout and Chars

Golden Trout

Cutthroat Trout

Brook Trout (Char)

Lake Trout (Char)

Dolly Varden Trout (Char)

Rainbow Trout

Brown Trout

26

Unlike the problem we had keeping the Black Basses sorted out, these aristocrats are easy. Just remember the spots and obvious markings. Have Dad study them and then run a quiz on him. And give him an "A", unless he should miss one. In that case, take him out and make him catch the one he missed!

Let's Teach Dad About Trout

Trout are a salmonoid fish (resembling Salmon). They belong to the same family of fishes: the Salmonidae. "Hey! Dad, I see you just caught a Salmo Trutta!"

If Bass are the criminal class, then the TROUT are the aristocrats. They are beautiful fish and I swear that they know it. Occasionally, you will find a very clear pool in a stream where you will be able to observe Trout. If it's an area where the Trout are accustomed to the movement of man, a condition quite common in, for example, a National Park, don't be surprised if it seems that the Trout watching you watching them seem to say with their movements; "See what a beautiful creature I am." You would have to be an expert-expert to catch Trout under this "You look at me, I look at you" condition. Just take the time with your Dad to observe them; he will learn a lot about Trout. After they have finished parading for you, settle down and watch quietly. If you sit long enough and quietly enough (I've sat at times for most of a day), they'll forget you are there and start leading the life of a Trout. Notice and point out to Dad:

• How they lie in the current facing upstream.
• All the spots that they have chosen for homes, like behind the rocks and the boulders.
• How they dart out for their food into the current or rise toward evening to the top for a dinner of insects.
• The sun overhead. (Do they seem affected by that? Do they move to the shade or an undercut bank? Well! They are smart as well as pretty. What would you do?)
• Do they feed all the time or rather at moments? (I guess to be honest, they prefer to feed when there is plenty of food. They don't seem to like to work too hard for a meal, which makes sense.) That is why mornings and particularly evenings are best;

TROUT • 27

that is when the food they prefer is most plentiful, the time of the hatch when the insects are thick and the Minnows are too.

The "hatch" refers to the emergence of aquatic insects, such as Mayflies, who live one stage of their lives, the nymph stage, below water. When the proper time arrives, the nymph swims to the surface and floats with the current. He then frees himself from his casing, called the "shuck." Now he becomes an insect with dull-colored wings, and he can fly. He is called at this point a "dun" or more scientifically a subimago. A day later the dun sheds its skin once again and is now an adult or an imago (called by most fishermen "spinner"). In a very short time the spinner will mate, deposit eggs, and die. Hundreds of species of Mayflies and Stoneflies go through this miraculous transformation; every day from early spring well into the fall sees another hatch.

Obviously, if you were to throw in a ton of the food that fish like at high noon . . . well, I imagine that they'd get plenty excited. Actually that ton of food happens naturally at times during the day, like after a heavy rainfall when all the worms and the bugs are washed down from the shore. It's a good time to fish during the day.

When they are scared and they run and you wait until all settles down once again, do the fish return to their favorite spots? Do fish that are larger seem to act differently than those that are small?

Have your Dad observe Trout with you for a while and then quiz him about the things discussed up above.

A good time for observation is after you've seen to it that your Dad has taken his limit of fish further upstream. It's a most pleasant way for the two of you to spend the evening before hitting the tent for the night.

Now for a little bad news:

Trout are not nearly so widespread or as adaptable as the Black Bass. Not everyone lives near Trout water. Trout must have faster and cleaner and colder water than Bass. Better Trout-fishing states have mountains. Ideal are rivers and streams that are fed by glaciers or spring-melted snow, or lakes that are high, where the water is cold. But the news isn't all bad. In fact, in a way it's quite bright. Trout are far more widespread today than they were back in their original wild time. This has happened because there are official programs of transporting and stocking these wonderful fish. (We can thank the fish and game departments of the various states, as well as interested sportsmen and clubs.) As part of these programs, many states with only marginal conditions that would support Trout have at least a put-and-take Trout-fishing situation. In fact, most of the Trout fished in the United States are populations of stocked and managed fish. More people than not, therefore, can enjoy at least some action on Trout. But you might have to travel a bit.

However, the Trout that we think of most and love best are those of the wild North country, and for those you might have to travel a *lot*.

The closest members of the family to Trout are the Chars, which we generally think of and speak of as Trout. We raise them as Trout, fish them as Trout, and love them for dinner as Trout. The difference between the Trout and the Char is all in the mouth—the vomer or bone on the roof of the mouth. Trout have teeth all along the length of this bone, while the Char have only a few teeth, toward the front of the bone. But there is an easier way to tell the two apart: and that is the spots. Generally the Trout has dark or black spots showing against a lighter body color, while the Char has light spots on a darker body color. You might also note that, as a rule, the Char prefer colder water than true Trout. Now, surprise Dad by telling him that one of our favorite "Trout," the native Brook Trout of the eastern United States is a Char. So, too, is the Dolly Varden Trout of the West, who was named after a character in the book *Barnaby Rudge* by Dickens. Dolly Varden wore a pink spotted dress and so does our Char.

So, start your Trout lessons with Dad by treating the Trout and the Char just alike.

The three most popular Trout are:

The RAINBOW TROUT
The BROWN TROUT
The BROOK TROUT (Char)

Others of more regional distribution that you might come to know and to love are:

The CUTTHROAT TROUT
The GOLDEN TROUT
The DOLLY VARDEN (Char)
The SUNAPEE TROUT
The LAKE TROUT (Char)
The GILA TROUT

There are also crossbreeds that happen in nature or as a result of select breeding at hatcheries, of which the most common are:
The BROWN-BOW (Brown Trout and Rainbow)
The CUT-BOW (Cutthroat and Rainbow)
TIGER TROUT (Brown Trout Female and Brook Trout Male)
The SPLAKE (Brook Trout and Lake Trout)
The Splake is the only one of these crosses that can reproduce itself. Think of the others as freshwater mules. (As you know, a mule is the offspring of a donkey and horse. Mules are sterile and cannot reproduce.)

All the Trout found in our country are not native to America. A

I've drawn pictures of the Trout and Chars for you on page 26.

good example is the Brown Trout, who comes to us from Europe. He was first introduced here in 1883. Brown Trout are now found on the East and West coasts and in all the Trout spots in between. They were also introduced to Asia, New Zealand, South America, and Africa. Mr. and Mrs. Brown Trout are far and away the smartest of our Trout. When you get Dad far enough along in his lessons, and he catches a Brown, compliment him roundly for doing everything right.

A native Trout of our country (in a way he's kind of Red, White and Blue) is the RAINBOW, who comes originally from our Pacific Northwest. He's also traveled quite a bit, almost as far as the Brown. He should be as smart, but for some reason he's not. I must admit, though, that when he is hooked he has more tricks than a barrel of Browns. He's a good jumper and head-shaker and he never gives up. You will find Rainbows in every state that has Trout. They are a favorite hatchery fish and adapt well to a wide variety of water conditions: lakes, ponds, big rivers, and small, even wee, creeks. If you happen to live out near his original home, the Northwest—in Northern California, Oregon, Washington, or parts of Idaho—you are likely to meet a Rainbow Trout that has spent part of his life in the sea, returning to the rivers and fresh water only to spawn (just like the Salmon you know all about). They are called STEELHEAD, and they are big, going as heavy as thirty-six pounds and they are *strong*. If you are blessed, and sometime find yourself and your Dad in a Steelhead state and unless (a happy surprise) we find that Dad is an expert on Steelhead and kept it a secret, I would suggest that you hire a guide. This is one fish about whom you have to know just when and where he is holding and waiting for you.

Now, to *my* own favorite of trouts: our BROOK TROUT—some call him "Square Tail" or "Native." By whatever name, he is beautiful and easy to recognize by his spots, which are spatters of yellow and some bright red, circled in blue. He is my favorite, perhaps, because he was the very first Trout I ever took on a fly, which you'll read about in the story I wrote about Trout. The Brook Trout prefers swift running water, streams that are clean and cold, more so than any other Trout, and because of this is not quite as widespread as the others. He is a native of the Northeast, more abundant in Canada, particularly Labrador, where he grows heavier in size than he is likely to in the States. But like his friends, he has traveled a bit and is found today in the West from the Rockies to other high mountains that reach to the sea. I have always found him at high altitudes in the West, in crystal-clear lakes that are snow-fed or in the runoff brooks from such lakes.

Some time or other you might hear an oldtimer in New England refer to a "Salter." He is talking about the Brook Trout, one who, like the Rainbow, will sometimes run to spend part of his life in the sea, but unlike the Rainbow (who grows heavy at sea) our Salter just doesn't. A four-pound or five-pound fish is a prize (the ones that stay home sometimes grow bigger).

The other grand Trout and the Chars that I've mentioned I'll not treat in detail in your book. They haven't traveled as far as the popular three: the Brown, the Rainbow, and the Brook. Why, some, like the Blueback Trout, are so rare that they're found in only a couple of ponds up in Maine—and even there are considered quite rare. In your fisherman's life, I hope you'll encounter them all, but by that time you will have made Dad an expert and you'll know all the Trout even better than I.

Let's get down to the Trout-fishing tricks you'll teach Dad:

First rule when going for Trout: *GO AS LIGHT AS YOU DARE.*

By that I mean, of course, your tackle. The most fun way to take Trout is with the *flyrod;* the easiest, *a spinning outfit.* I'll discuss the spinning rod first and leave the choice up to you. You'll know the best way after you've read the chapter on each.

As I said, spinning is easy. A novice-fisherman father can learn to cast like an expert in almost no time at all. This is a plus, because he will think that he's smart (which, as you know, he probably is). And, because he is smart and will listen to you, he should start taking fish right away which, after all, is what makes the sport fun. He'll want to go fishing more often and will learn twice as fast.

Another plus to consider is cost. A truly top spinning outfit will cost a lot less than a really good fly outfit. Good spinning outfits are rugged and serve well under almost any condition you'll run into when fishing for Trout. You can narrow your choice of lures to just two or three that will always take Trout. (Now, if you insist on knowing about flyrods at this point, turn to page 38 and run through what's said there.)

But back to the *lightness* of tackle. Most of the Trout that you'll meet will weigh less than two pounds. Gear up for them and use *ultra light gear:* a rod that weighs three ounces or less, and a monofilament line of no more than three pounds of test. Two pound test is even better. You can land surprisingly large fish with this little outfit, for the small reel you use will be equipped with a drag that is nothing more or less than a brake built into the mechanical reel. It allows a heavy and strong fish to strip out line up to the point of a predetermined tension (drag) that you manually set; the tension is below the breaking point of your line. Without this drag almost any fish would quickly break your light line.

Tell your Dad to keep it set light and until he's an expert not to play too much with the drag. Tell him, while we are about this business of lightness, that he *should* expect fish to break off occasionally . . . you know, using cobwebs to fish with and all (it's part of the fun). Tell him not to get upset or to mind it. Tell him to be patient, as, pretty soon, for every fish that he's lost he'll be taking three. If you need to prove this point to him about lightness, tell him to go on ahead and to fish with a line that tests out six or eight pounds in a lake that you know has some good Trout. You stick to your little light line and outfish him at least five to one. If the day is just right you'll never be able to count all the strikes that you'll have.

In most Trout waters where it's quiet, at early morning or evening you will see the Trout feeding. They rise to the surface to feed on the hatch (insects) dappling the water. This is the good time to be fishing, but be quiet and smooth and think light. Have your Dad cast out from the shore where you have seen the Trout rising and have him start his lure immediately back . . . rather slow . . . just enough speed for the action. Chances are he'll be into a Trout before you can say, "I've got one!!" If nothing should happen within a few casts, have him vary the speed of retrieve, a little bit either faster or slower. Also, let him give some thought to the depth. Sometimes if your lure sinks a little bit deeper you'll find all the action. Also, remember to remind Dad about the walking I told you to do. Walk along the shore of the lake ten feet or so and then cast. The same advice, in many ways, applies to the rivers: some are so large you'll be on the bank, while on others you'll wade looking for the most likely spots as you move. Continue as far as you want to or can go.

Prove to Dad that he can take Trout at midday too. You won't see them rising as a general rule, but you can find them. Remember when we had a fish at your place at the table . . . burger and all? Well, now is the time to trade places and imagine yourself in the place of the fish.

A lot of the rules apply that applied when you were looking for Bass. Look for the dropoffs and holes. Look for logs or whatever that it would be fun to hide behind in the shade; if you were a fish, you might head for an undercut bank or a cave where it's cool. At the moment we are talking of lakes. Now, in your walks, did you find where the river or stream comes pouring in, feeding the lake? Well, you as a fish would know that this is also the spot that is feeding you all sorts of goodies washed down from the hills. If you know of springs in the lake, these are really good spots, for, as a rule, they are in the deeper parts of the lake. Fresh water and cool springs stir up and attract all sorts of food.

Now—if you were a fish in a stream: Think! What spots would you likely hang out in? Of course, you would choose the more fishy and most interesting spots. It's funny but true, you as a person think a lot like a fish. For example, when you stand on the shore and stare at a river or stream, your eye and your interest are pulled to the river's most interesting parts, like the rock where the stream swirls or a tree that went down with a flood and now lies in midstream, the waterfall or the pool or the calm on either side of a race, or there where the river junctions or joins another river or flow. These are the spots that you naturally seek out; they are different and appeal to the eye. They appeal to fish too. You as a

The Lake: Both Bass and Trout like the same general qualities of a lake. Use this as a guide for both species.

sunken grass beds

feeder stream (inlet)

course of old river bed

sand or gravel bar

underwater spring

rocky dropoff

submerged reef

usually the deeper area of the lake

debris (logs and sunken trees)

(outlet)

dam

floating vegetation

Grassy banks are good places to fish.

Trout love logs and fallen trees to hide under

behind rocks and obstructions

Fishing under and around bridges and structures is often excellent.

undercut bank (for Big Brown Trout, particularly)

The River

a pool at the foot of a waterfall

Look for fish around gravel and sand bars. (The downstream end would be favored.)

33

fish would wait behind those boulders and snags that cause eddies that trap all your food. You will be facing upstream, into the current, so you can see what's coming your way. Of course, if you were as smart as a Brown Trout (hardly anyone is), you'd hide in an under-cut bank where you'd never be seen and take time looking over every surprise floating by. You would really have to be fooled in the most subtle of ways—you'd never jump out at an anchor—but you just might jump out for something you thought was a dinner . . . if it was tied to a very, very light line.

You will have noticed by now that I stress tackle that's light. I do so because I consider that of the utmost importance if you are to get your Dad out and right into fish and, most importantly, fun.

There is, of course, another reason, one that you probably already know but have never thought of; of course that reason is *you*, at least if *you* are like most young teachers I've met. You will go fishing with dreams of huge fighting monsters and, quick as you are on your feet, you will want to go out *really* prepared. Well, that is Jim Dandy all right and a good old American trait; but think for a moment how lucky you are to have a whole bag full of other equally wonderful American traits that lend themselves easily to the sport. Let me tell you a story about the time when I was learning this teaching trade and discovered the advantages of using light line. Without any prompting, I hope you'll recognize a few American traits.

There was a time when I didn't believe in using light lines. It was almost "the heavier, the better for me." After all, who wants a fish to bust off and take hook and line with him?

I used to spend entirely too much time down at Tucker's Sporting Goods store (occasionally they'd remind me of that fact). But it was serious business for me—deciding on lines. I would spend hours mulling over the cheapest and heaviest lines they carried in stock. The one I eventually chose as my favorite had some name or other that suggested the sea: "Brine Air," or "Wave Crest," perhaps even "Rip Tide." It was something like that. The thing about it that impressed me was the line's color, wretched dull and dark green. It came spooled on a white wooden spool that helped add further presumptions to the green. Clearly marked on the spool was the proud guarantee: "This line has a warranted wet breaking strength of about 90 & 105 pounds." I had no doubt but that it did. It also felt slightly fuzzy beneath the thumb, a fact that I found reassuring, for I had an unbounded faith in "our" manufacturing know-how.

It was also competitively priced at 19¢ per 25 yards, which, while shooting a large hole in my tackle budget, was still within reach of my pocket.

"I'll take this here twenty-five yards," I told Mr. Tucker. I paid and headed out for the bridge. Needless to say, excitement was high in my soul; new lines tend to add an edge. I was enjoying the thought that there were no fish in the sea who would be a match for my line. And in that I was right, at least where I fished, for I caught a couple of fine Sheepshead which I didn't even realize that I'd caught until they came out of the water. I later realized that both had given up whatever fight they had planned when they first felt the weight of that soggy wet line.

I on the other hand gave up heavy line for intellectual reasons. A tourist from some far northern state, who was fishing a few elbows away, stumbled in ignorance onto something I have been able to use with delightful effect all of my life.

It happened this way: When I noticed the tourist, and his light little freshwater bass outfit, with line I know couldn't test more than maybe ten pounds wet breaking strength, I felt like laughing aloud at anything so dumb. But being by nature wholly compassionate, I gave him my pity instead.

"That there rig of yours is going to get all bonkered up by these here fish. . . . Florida fish are real fighting fish!" I told him, hoping that I could be of some help. It was just about that time (I think) that I caught the second Sheepshead, a Florida fish that didn't exactly punctuate my statement as graphically as I would have hoped.

But both the best and the worst of our short relationship happened about the same time; just then that poor tourist fellow lucked into a fighting Spanish Mackerel that went an easy seven pounds. That light little line of his cut through the water and literally sang. The fish was all over the place, rolling and flashing in the sunlight and throwing spray almost as high as the rail of the bridge. The excitement was contagious, and a crowd of fishermen gathered around shouting advice. But because I knew this fellow the best, I shouted the loudest (trying to ease the letdown that I knew surely would come when what would happen, would happen). "That old fish gonna bust that line to ribbons! . . . That Florida fish's gonna bust that little old rod into splinters," I yelled.

Of course that fellow was lucky, and he managed in time (twenty minutes or so) to walk along the bridge to the beach and bring that beautiful fish up onto the shore. Everyone crowded around and congratulated him and told him what a fine fight he had made. Naturally I, too, felt a great deal of pride in the outcome. Well, for one thing, I was the one who had been closest throughout the fight and therefore could answer some of the questions that came from the crowd. I also felt that some of my cautions were responsible for that fellow fighting as hard as he did. But mostly I was proud that I had been proved so right about Florida fish, which even the lucky fisherman himself felt compelled to tell me just before I left on my bike and headed back down to Tucker's to see if Mr. Tucker would be willing to trade me a new lighter line with a better guarantee.

One of our best traits of all: To admit we are wrong when we *are* wrong!

Some advice about lures for your spinning:

I won't list the thousands of kinds of lures that are made, though many, I'm sure, are quite good. Instead, I'll list only a few that will always take Trout. There's more on this subject in our section on Tackle.

My two favorites are mepps and rapalas.

The *mepps* are small spinners of various size and design, most of which are quite good. My favorite models for the lakes are the Mepps Aglia longs in size one or two, made of brass. For smaller streams and brooks I prefer the same models in sizes zero and one.

Rapalas are plugs that look like minnows. We shall use the small size for Trout. I personally like the "sinking" models for lakes and large streams, models CD-5 and CD-7 in silver, though gold is good some of the time. For the smaller streams and rivers I prefer the floating models in silver, size 5.

Other lures that I think are good when fishing for Trout (because of my two favorites I seldom use anything else) are small *spoons* like the Dardevle (red and white) in a small size: ¼ oz. or ½ oz.

There's Wob-l-rite in the same size range (I like this one in gold) and, likewise in gold, I like Phoebe, another small spoon, shaped like a fish.

Two others I like, though I have no idea as to what natural Trout food they represent (thank goodness the Trout know!): the *flatfish* in orange and black (small spinning size) and *super-duper,* which is a kind of spoon but not quite.

With most of these lures, cast slightly upstream and across; let the flow of the water do some of the work. You'll soon get the feel. Sometimes, if the water is deep enough to permit it, try casting upstream and swim your lure back at a fast-enough speed to impart action. On the lakes, of course, just work straight ahead, occasionally varying your depth. A secret that generally works well for me, so tell it to Dad, is to start your retrieve the instant your lure hits the water. Even a Trout who might have been spooked by the cast doesn't have time to worry too much; he just hears the plunk and sees dinner starting to run.

By the way, a bit of advice:

Most of the lures that I've talked about are really so good they have been copied—and usually much cheaper. Resist the temptation to buy these "bargains," for I assure you the fish too will resist the "cheap" copies.

Don't be afraid to find favorites yourself. There are many fine lures I've not listed, many I've not even tried to catch fish with. Just be thankful that you will never let your Dad down by suggesting the ones I have listed.

I've sketched a few of my favorite Trout spinning lures for you.

two types of Mepps

Rapala

Dardevle

Flatfish

Wob-l-rite

WOB-L-RITE

Super-duper

Phoebe

Fly Fishing for Trout

I certainly hope at this point that you have been able to teach your Dad quite a bit about Trout. Usually the job isn't too difficult, as you may already have noticed when you showed him a picture of a Trout leaping. Now, ask him a question: "Hey, Dad, do you know why that old trout is leaping?"

Watch out for a "smart"-father answer like: "Well, Son, I reckon he's restless (or dancing or trying out for the team)." They throw those kind of answers once in awhile (to see if you'll smile).

Hey! Go ahead, smile, nod your head wisely, and say: "Gee Dad, you're smart—that's a gasser of an answer."

Now, he'll smile, and that's when you give him the works. For example, you say: "Well, judging from all of the clues in the picture, I'd say it's early season . . . the water is high . . . there are patches of snow and the trees are just budding. The water looks cold and it's fast. I should say it's probably then, most likely, stonefly in a limited hatch (stoneflies usually hatch early season). I would say it's a good time to fly fish a *nymph* or *dun* of that bug. That's why he's leaping." At this point, fathers usually stop smiling and start listening. You now have his fullest attention.

Good. You've just started your Dad on his first steps to fly fishing for Trout which, besides being the best of the sport, is also an art and a science: observation and knowledge of insects is the key. Tell Dad that at least 90 percent of a Trout's food is made up of insects, and that what we are going to do is to fool him with bug imitations made of feathers and furs and some tinsel.

That certainly is simple, except:

Tell your Dad that if he wants to be good at this sport he must *match* his knowledge of bugs with that of the Trout, which every fisherman knows is pretty darn good. A Trout understands exactly what species of insect is and should be about, under any and every condition. He seldom will bother with or take anything else: if he's feeding on gnats, he wants gnats and not moths; when it's the time of the year for mayflies, that's what he wants and he will turn down a grasshopper fake, no matter how pretty it may look to you. (Whoever heard of a pretty grasshopper? Dad's answer, of course, "Another grasshopper.")

I think you might see now why I've called this wonderful sport partially a *science*. It involves a study of bugs, but don't be discouraged. We'll keep it so simple for Dad that in no time at all he'll be yelling: "Go get the rods; there's a hatch!" Which is better than "Go get a swatter; there's bugs!"

Let's leave the bugs to the Trout for a while and talk about *art.* Tell Dad that the art we mean, besides all the beauty he'll find, is the art of the use of the fly rod. If you have ever seen a picture of, in fact ever actually seen, a fly rod in use over a stream, you probably have marveled at the grace of the line as it moves back and forth on the cast. You have also probably thought to yourself, "I wish I could do that . . . but it looks pretty hard." Well, it is and it isn't; mostly it isn't. Just explain to your Dad that he needs the right *line* and right *rod*.

Let's teach him some fisherman's language.

The right rod, or a good one to start with, would be a rod of about seven and one-half to eight feet length—one that weighs 3⅞ oz. (approximate weight)—designed to handle a DT—6—F line. How's that for some fisherman's language? Explain to your Dad what it means.

There are balanced fly tackle standards set down in code so that each maker of tackle and each fisherman knows what is meant. It's really quite simple.

Let's start with the line: DT—6—F. The DT stands for *D*ouble *T*aper (wasn't that hard?). The 6 stands for the weight of the line, as follows:

#1 — weight 60 grains (a grain is a unit of weight, like one grain of wheat. Look it up! You will find that it's .002 of an ounce or .0648 gram)
#2 — 80 grains
#3 — 100 grains
#4 — 120 grains
#5 — 140 grains
#6 — 160 grains   This is the line we are using: #6.
#7 — 185 grains
#8 — 210 grains
#9 — 240 grains
#10 — 280 grains
#11 — 330 grains
#12 — 380 grains

So explain to Dad that, so far, we know that we have a line that is double tapered and weighs 160 grains.

The *F* stands for Floating. Tell Dad. Hurrah! he has a double tapered line that weighs 160 grains, and it *floats*. You might also further explain that the double taper means that your line tapers down to a smaller diameter at both ends (the body or belly of the line is a little bit thicker). Use either end; it's reversible (that's a plus: the same applies to a level line, one of uniform thickness).

Other codes about lines that you might as well explain to your Dad are

WF and *L* and *S*.
The *WF* stands for Weight Forward
The *L* stands for Level.
and the *S* is for Sinking.

Your code line might have read WF—6—S. Weight forward 160 grains, and it sinks. Or it might have read L—7—F: level line of 185 grains, and it floats.

But the line that we have chosen, the DT—6—F is just about perfect for beginning on fly fishing for Trout.

You might have gathered by now just how important the line is in fly fishing. Well it certainly is! For when fly casting, you are casting *the weight of the line* as opposed to, for example, when out spinning you were casting the weight of the lure. Just make sure that your Dad's fly line and the rod are in balance. Most manufacturers list the weight of the line that their rod was designed to carry right on the rod itself.

Fly rods are made of three principal materials: bamboo, graphite, and fiberglass.

Good bamboo rods, designed by the masters, are extremely expensive. Graphite rivals bamboo in both action and cost.

Fiberglass rods are the ones that most of us use. If they are made by a manufacturer who really cares about his reputation, they can be very good indeed. See the chapter on Tackle, page 205.

Now that Dad has assembled his rod and chosen his line, it is time for you to explain about reels. Tell Dad that the reel for his fly fishing outfit is really (but reely) quite unimportant. Explain that unlike all other rod-and-reel fishing, the reel here is used only to store line. Tell him to remember his *line hand* he will be stripping fish in; seldom is it necessary to "play" the fish from the reel. Of course, there are exceptions, for example when he's hooked up a very large fish (this doesn't happen very often with Trout, we'll talk about this later when we move on to Salmon and Steelhead or saltwater fishing). Anyway, almost any old flyreel will do, as long as it's large enough to store the line with a little bit of regular fishing line as backing, which probably should be there just in case he might hook that extra large Trout. The reel for fly fishing can be quite inexpensive (which is good.)

Casting:

Now, before we talk about the business end of his outfit (the leader and fly), let's send Dad out for some practice at casting. This he can do any old place—the backyard or a field—any place where he has room for his cast. Don't try to put a fly and its hook on at this point, as he'll only catch trees and/or you (which slows down your lesson).

Now, casting is the part that looks hard. It is not. Of course, it might seem awkward at first, but if Dad can hop on one foot, wave his arms in the air, and shout, "Come and get it, Old Trout!" then he's ready to learn.

First, string up the outfit (run the line through the guides). Then, hold out your hands and say to your Dad, if he's right-handed, as you raise your right hand: "Your right hand is your *rod hand*." Now, hold up your left hand and explain: "Your left hand is your *line hand*." Tell him it's used for stripping and hauling (pulling line off or in). Okay—now have him relax and stand easy as if he was just talking to you—and he probably will. He might even ask, "Okay;

now what do I do?" (Never let questions like that throw you. Simply step back and make an appraisal. You might even add a "Hmmmm!" as you study his posture.)

"Well, you're certainly right-handed!" you say, and then add, "Favor your weight on your right leg; keep your left foot slightly out front." (This is quite likely how he will stand anyway, even without your advice; most right-handed people do so when they relax while on their feet.)

The next thing you do is strip off about fifteen to twenty feet of line through the guides and stretch it out in front of him. Once again tell him to relax; you might even tell him it helps to think of big fish (some fathers can do this quite easily right in the backyard).

Have him grip the rod firmly, keeping his thumb on top of the grip. Then, have him hold the rod out in front, his elbow comfortably bent, the tip of the rod about level with his eyes. Tell him that his wrist should be *stiff* and remain so; explain that his arm should feel like an extension of the rod or, better still, if you wish, tell him to feel the rod as part of his arm. (As you know, any piece of equipment that you use often and well seems to be part of you; think of your bike, skate board, or skates.)

Now you say: "The following is done very sharply and *smoothly* (stress smoothly). Think of using a hammer; bend your arm at the elbow, bringing your rod up and back. You want your fist to come up right near your ear (but don't hit it; that would look silly). When your rod is straight up (think of twelve o'clock), pause; actually come to a brief stop. Your fly line will move through the air, up and behind you (this is called the *back cast*). Now your line straightens out to the rear. When you feel it start to tug at your rod tip (it's the weight of the line that does it), bring your arm down through the same arc that it took going up. Again it should be a smooth and sharp drive (think of driving a nail with a hammer). Keep your wrist stiff and press with your thumb and don't be surprised as your weight shifts ever so slightly to your forward left leg, for it should. If everything so far is done smoothly, your line has shot out on its way to a trout (at least in your Dad's mind) and the *forward cast* is completed."

You might take the time to explain what lies ahead when you take him afield, put him in waders, and stand him in midstream. He will be fighting a current and slippery rocks. Once again have him relax, and explain to him that the first order of business is safe and sure footing (you don't want him to fall and scare all the Trout). He will worry about maintaining the proper stance and weight distribution. Tell him not to worry, that he will find himself adjusting and shifting his weight, bracing a foot here or there, and still he will wind up, as if by some magic, in his most comfortable casting position. Tell him not to be stiff, to go ahead and look around. He should feel free enough to look back over his shoulder to see what his back cast is up to. Does it straighten out properly? Are there trees or even people to watch out for? (It doesn't pay to catch people

Look at the illustrations on the next pages.

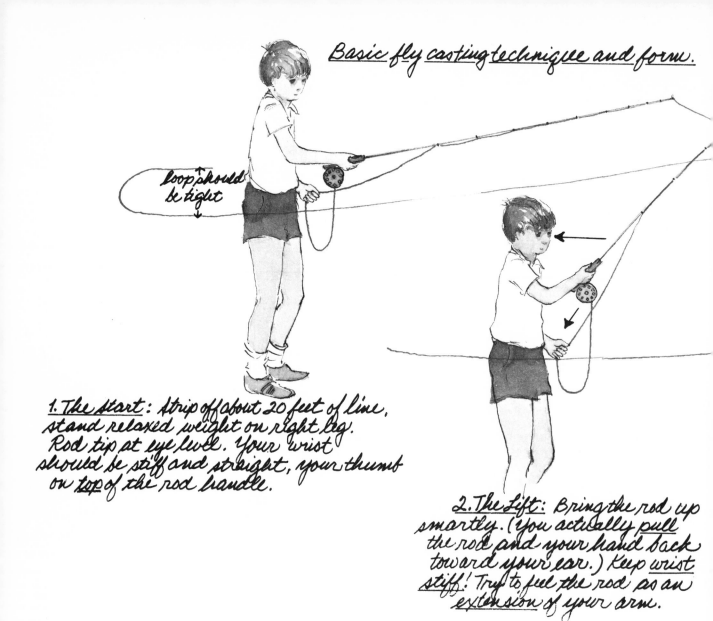

Basic fly casting technique and form.

loop should be tight

1. The start: Strip off about 20 feet of line, stand relaxed weight on right leg. Rod tip at eye level. Your wrist should be stiff and straight, your thumb on top of the rod handle.

2. The Lift: Bring the rod up smartly. (You actually pull the rod and your hand back toward your ear.) Keep wrist stiff! Try to feel the rod as an extension of your arm.

5. Release the line with your line hand and the line should "shoot" out, completing your cast and catching a trout (or at least a piece of the lawn).

line hand

42

3. Stop at about the eleven o'clock position. Feel free to look back over your shoulder at the line. (It really pays to study what is happening on your backcast.) Notice the cane effect just before your line straightens out. (It should be "tight", just as I have shown it.) Just before it _straightens_, _power_ your forward stroke. (Remember the hammer.)

The "cane" loop, as you complete the forward cast, should mirror the one on your back cast.

should be tight

4. The forward cast: As your line starts to travel forward, really apply pressure with your thumb. Try to aim your hand at the target — the rod tip will follow — if you've kept that wrist stiff!

43

or trees; that will ruin your fly!) In fly casting you have plenty of time to look to the rear, avoid all the problems, and then turn forward, pick out a target, and hit it right on the nose. (That, too, is quite automatic.) Your Dad will be quite proud of how accurate he is with a fly rod. Give him a round of applause and avoid pointing out that accuracy with this type of rod is as simple as slowly pointing your finger at something.

Keep him at practice until he feels that it all is quite natural; soon he will be *false casting*, that is, keeping his line in the air for a number of passes back and forth before he decides to drop it down out in front. Usually, when you see a fisherman false casting he's not showing off, though it looks mighty pretty. What he is doing is drying (shaking) the water out of his lure so it'll float like a bug when it lands.

Tell Dad that what we've discussed are simply the basics of casting and quite good enough to take plenty of Trout. Most of his casts for taking Trout will be short ones, twenty to thirty feet out. Tell him not to extend himself or to try to get fancy until it's all second nature, and then he will learn lots of tricks for himself.

Study the sketches of casting.

Leaders and Flies:

Now is the time to talk to your Dad about leaders and flies. (He should be ready for his first fly fishing trip.) The fly leader is almost as important as the line, for it is the leader that must complete the cast and carry your energy right out to the fly, turning the fly over and landing it correctly and gently like a real bug putting down. To do this the leader is tapered; the section that joins the line is called the butt (the thicker, heavier end). This tapers at the tip or the tippet, which is the light business-end where you tie on your fly. Leaders for fly fishing are long; the average is about 9 feet. Anything from there down to 7½ feet is considered quite short; anything over 10 feet would be long. Tell Dad at first to buy all his leaders—there are very good ones already balanced and tapered; the only thing that is important to know about leaders at this point in his education are the codes that give the strength and the size of the tip or tippet. Again, I remind you to go as light as you dare. A light leader, as with the light spinning line, will fool many more fish.

The code is a number-plus-"X" code. The higher the number, the lighter the tip. For Trout we would be interested only in the higher numbers like 3X to 7X. Here's how they rate:

CODE	DIAMETER	TEST (in lbs.)
OX	.011	9.0
1X	.010	7.8
2X	.009	7.0

CODE	DIAMETER	TEST (in lbs.)
3X	.008	5.3
4X	.007	3.5
5X	.006	2.5
6X	.005	1.8
7X	.004	1.0

5X, 6X, 7X are good normal choices for Trout. Just remember that the lower and clearer the water, the smaller you will have to go. Tell Dad that he can land surprisingly large fish on these light leaders if he is gentle.

Now to the flies . . . and hooray for them!

Let's try to keep this rather complicated part of the business as simple as possible. After all, if your Dad is as good a student as you are, he'll go on ahead and read books and learn as much as he can by himself. What you as his teacher want him to do right away is to take enough beautiful fish to keep him happier than you ever thought he could be. (When you see him give a big smile, you will know that even he didn't believe it.)

There are basically two types of flies: dry fly and wet fly.

The *wet fly* is by far the easiest to fish. Tell your Dad that wet flies represent insects of various kinds, as well as Minnows or small crustaceans, such as the Scud or freshwater Shrimp. Often a single wet fly pattern can represent anyone or all of these; it depends on how it is fished. For example, if fished with a darting action it could well be a Minnow, or if with similar darting action and close to the bottom, it might seem like a Shrimp. If free-floating, its action, if any, imparted by the current might make it seem an insect or nymph. Wet flies are, therefore, good most of the time and will almost always take fish. With wet flies, as far as I'm concerned, it's a matter of trying a variety of patterns until you find one that the fish like as well as you do. A few of the patterns you might recommend to your Dad are:

Turn back to pages 24 - 25 to study the pictures of flies I've drawn for you.

Hendrickson (the *Light* or the *Dark*)
Gordon and the *Quill Gordon*
Stonefly
Light Cahill or *Campbells Fancy*
March Brown or *Iron Blue Dun*
Yellow Sally and *Professor* are good when you feel lighter and brighter

There are two other flies that are fished wet. Each of these represents a particular food for the trout:
The streamers and the nymphs.

The *Streamers* represent Minnows, some of which are quite colorful. They should be fished rather fast, with action imparted by stripping in line: when they are darting, the action is just about

Light Hendrickson

gordon

Stonefly

Light Cahill

Campbells Fancy

march Brown

Iron Blue Dun

Yellow Sally

Professor

right. You don't need a big collection of these. Just a few in dark patterns and a few in light. Sometimes the fish will prefer one or the other.

Recommend to Dad the following patterns:

Dark Tiger, Light Tiger
Nine-Three and *Nite Owl*
Wardens Worry or *White Maribou Streamer*

Suggest to your Dad that he try streamers early season or when the water is high. Also remember, because they represent Minnows, Dad will have a shot at a pretty big Trout.

Streamers of a special type that look to me to be designed halfway between the nymphs and the Minnows are the *Muddler* and the *Spuddler*. Both are excellent, and I always carry both patterns, sometimes they will take fish when nothing else will.

The Nymphs:

Here is a fly that is fished underwater, which makes it a *wet.* As the name implies this is designed to look like the nymph stage of an insect. The nymphs are probably the most effective lures for the fly rodder. They are made to match any number of insects . . . if and a great big *IF* . . . they match the nymph of the day and the season. Remember Trout are SMART! *They will not be fooled* (often) by a Stonefly Nymph that seems to be active and hatching fully two months late and right in the middle of, say, a Mayfly hatch. Carry a selection of nymphs that represent a few of the important naturals. Ask for and buy only the best imitations of the Stonefly Nymph and the Mayfly Nymph, the Caddis Fly Nymph, the Dragonfly Nymph. Of all the fly types, it is most necessary that the nymph look as if it could really crawl away. Trout have time to examine a nymph, and they want something that really looks real.

There is also a trick to hooking a fish with a nymph. Nymphs are fished (as a rule) by casting upstream as with the dry fly and letting the lure tumble naturally back to you. Do not impart any action, as most of the nymphs when in the act of rising from the bottom just seem to float upward, swimming hardly at all (the dragonfly nymph is an exception: he can really move along). The Trout will take the imitation quite slowly in mouth, and you will see or feel only the slightest of drags to the float, maybe just a perceptible pause. You must strike and hope for the best: lift your rod tip up smartly with a flick of your wrist and hope you're surprised with a fish and not with a snag. Nymph fishing is difficult because it takes great timing and knowledge, but if you can get your Dad into it he'll like it a lot.

The Dry Fly

This is the type of fly that most people think of when they think of fly fishing, and with good reason. There are even fishermen who think so highly of this form of fly fishing that they fish only with the floating fly; they consider themselves "purists" and tend to look down their noses at any other form of the sport. Well, I don't agree and I'm not quite convinced that many of the purists do either, at least deep down inside. Many's the time I've strolled past one of these guys and watched his eyes cross as he looks down his nose and sees the Trout that I took on a nymph, a Trout bigger than anything he's seen in two years. I've a hunch that somewhere in one of the boxes in which he carries his flies he'll find something that looks like a nymph and soon will be back to the action with a smile and wild hopes. I really admire the thought of the purist, however, and have even thought of myself as one at times in the past. There are certainly a number of things to say about the single-minded pursuit of the Trout with a dry.

1. This is the most gentle form of the art of fly fishing. It is also perhaps the most lonely. You'll need your own stretch of stream, since Trout rising to feed are easily "put down" if there is too much splashing and/or lines flying about.

2. If you like the challenge of learning (and who doesn't?), then this is the sport. Fishing the dry requires more knowledge of flies than any other form of the sport. The imitations tied for the dry overshadow all other forms in sheer numbers of patterns.

3. If you love to read, you are lucky. The literature devoted to fishing the dry fly is truly quite beautiful and inspiration enough to carry you through more than one lifetime of fishing.

I guess these alone are reasons enough to be a purist, but for heavens' sake don't ever look down your nose. There's the danger that your eyes will come crossed and you'll never be able to tie on a dry fly again.

HOORAY FOR DRY FLY FISHERMEN! Tell Dad that this is what he must learn to take fish at this sport.

Dry flies represent all manner of forms of the insect that man in his wisdom has learned that Trout will feed on: spiders and ants, flies and bees and beetles (singing and nonsinging kinds), mosquitos and gnats (also, I suspect, hummingbirds and low-flying bats). The most important of the insects are, of course, the aquatic types, those that are born and/or hatched in the water. (Lucky for us, this narrows the choice to a few thousand or so.) But don't go getting discouraged: once again, keep it simple. Reason out that there are major hatches of insects during the season. Have your Dad concentrate on these; there is quite a history behind them and they are proven to work. Dry flies don't always have to look exactly like what they are cracked up to be. The size and the color alone are often enough to fool even the smartest of Trout. After all, Friend Trout is really looking up at a mirror, which is what the surface of the water looks like to him. Anything that sits up there properly, about the right size and right shape, can certainly fool him. Because the Trout really can't see too much of the fly on the float, it's better to buy types rather than patterns. I would guess that no more than eight or nine types are needed on most of our Trout streams. These eight or

Dark Tiger

Nine Three

Nite Owl

Warden's Worry

White Maribou

Dan Bailey Muddler

Spuddler

Hendrickson Nymph

Long tail Marde Brown Nymph

the "Teeny" Nymph

TROUT • 47

Irresistible

Iron Blue Dun

Royal Coachman (Hairwing)

Royal Coachman (Fanwing)

Grey Wulff

Adams

Light Cahill

nine types then would be tied in hundreds of patterns, so tell Dad just to buy types. Start by thinking the smallest; these would be gnats. When gnats are tied on very small hooks, like number 18s or 20s, they will do nicely for any number of insects that you hardly can see. The higher the number, the smaller the hook (opposite the way line works): # 20 is smaller than # 18. As a rule, dry flies are tied on smaller and lighter hooks than are streamers and wets. (Check the section on tackle in the back of the book: p. 205.) These flies should be fished when you see Trout rising and you can't make out what they are feeding on; be assured it's one of a number of very small gnats. Other types besides the gnat that you and your Dad should carry would be spiders and hairwings, divided wings and down wings, fan wings and bi-visibles. Always remember, before you make any decisions about the type of fly you might use, study what's happening around you and try to match the most numerous and common insect you see. If you really get stumped, try out a well-tied mosquito; they're always around (darn it!).

Anyway, with a dozen or so flies in your fly box or stuck in your hat, you are in pretty good shape—any place in the country. Always check, when you can, with local fly fishing experts about what they think is out flying and feeding the Trout.

Try to explain to your Dad (he'll understand it at once) that dry flies are usually fished upstream so they'll float down back to you with almost no drag. Just keep stripping in line as it floats. *Don't pull it,* simply keep up with it, so that your line is under control. Make a few casts and then keep working upstream. Go quietly; always pretend that you are sneaking up on the Trout. Keep your eyes open and *watch out for holes. Study your bugs* and then give the Trout what you know he will like. You'll like it too.

Recommend to your Dad the following patterns in drys:

IRRESISTIBLE on a # 12 or # 14 hook
IRON BLUE DUN on a # 12 or # 14 hook
ROYAL COACHMAN HAIRWING on a # 12 # 14 # 16
ROYAL COACHMAN FANWING on a # 12 # 14 # 16
GREY WULFF on a # 12 & # 14
ADAMS on a # 12 & # 14
LIGHT CAHILL on a # 12 & # 14
MOSQUITO on a # 12 thru # 16
WHITE WULFF on a # 12 thru # 14
BROWN BI-VISIBLE on a # 12 thru # 14
ATHERTON # 6 on a # 12 # 14 & # 16
BLACK GNAT on a # 16 # 18 & # 20

Reviews and Hints for Trout

1. Trout require a very light touch. They are shy.

2. Trout fishing will be only as good as your lure. Trout are smart,

not easily fooled. Use only the best in hand-tied flies, or tie your own very carefully. Good spinning lures are expensive, but they pay off with more fish and more fun.

3. Think of the water as the home of the Trout. Read it and know just where he'll be waiting for food.

4. When afoot, give the area a good working-over—walking and casting—but remember that, in each spot, just a few casts—two or three—are enough either to take fish or put them down for a while. *Once again,* they are smart. You be as smart and move on too.

5. Trout tend to "sink" as air temperature rises, so go deeper when the weather gets warm.

6. Early morning and *evenings* are best.

7. The spring and the fall are the best Trout times of the year. Summer's okay, but as a rule you'll have to go higher upland, like the mountains where the water is cool.

8. When you've brought your Dad to the point where he's an expert, taking Trout on a regular basis, stress *sportsmanship* (when you are good, it's most of the fun). Introduce him to barbless hooks and see that he releases most of his fish. Keep only those that you'll share for your dinner.

9. A new thought to remember: It is supposed that all fishermen *fib*. This is simply not true. Only *bad* fishermen fib. Good fishermen live their fish stories each trip. When they tell stories of the big ones that broke off, the stories are true. Or the ones that they took and let go; those too are true. So keep an eye on your Dad. When he stops fibbing, you'll know that you've done your job well, and he's good.

mosquito

White Wulff

Brown Bivisible

Atherton 6

Black Gnat

A Story About Trout

When you've been fishing awhile, you will find that you own and enjoy thousands of stories, things that have happened to you, such is the case with myself. I'm sure that you remember the story of my meeting my very first Black Bass when I was eight (a wood-eating fish, indeed). Well now I shall tell you the story of my first meeting a Trout.

I was grown-up and wiser, struggling with age, which was 14, an age that has its plus side as anyone knows who's been through it. For one, you're no longer afraid of the pirates, while the cannibals are shunted to the rear of your mind, only vaguely a fear, and that because of their pots and your knowledge of Bass. As to rivers, you've lost all apprehension. You take them, explore them, and love them as each comes along. I don't intend to imply that, because I was aged and wise when I first met the Trout, there was nothing that gnawed at my soul, for there was. Along with the cannibals that lived in the back of my mind was a haunt and a fear and some guilt that dealt with the concept of flyrods. That may seem strange to you who already fish, but please note: I was a Florida boy, and flyrods were designed to take Salmon and Trout, neither of which chose to live in my wonderful native state.

You might say, "That is no reason for a feeling of guilt." Well, I suppose you are right, except that I once owned a flyrod: a Payne. Now a Payne was a rod of perfection, built of bamboo by a man named Payne. I should say that, if you went out to buy one today, you would have to mortgage the house. Anyway, I once owned a Payne, bequeathed to me, when I was still in my sniveling years, by an uncle up north (rest his good soul). This story undoubtedly will bring a tear to the eye of the true devotee of the fly fishing sport, not because of my uncle, but because of my Payne.

It "got busted" the first afternoon that I snuck it out for a fish. The culprit (not I) was a very small Jack, which because of his size went to confirm what we Florida boys knew in those days, and I quote: "Them funny-looking long rods are for sissies . . . they ain't no good for Florida fish." This I know now is very, very untrue. But I gave it a heave into the deep of the bay and smiled to be rid of so impractical an invention. Six years later, when I first learned about Trout and about flyrods on a chill and beautiful stream in Connecticut I almost started to snivel again. You talk about guilt . . . you talk about pain. We were visiting up north, my Father and I, "reviewing the scene," as he said. It was spring and Trout season was open; only natural that I should give him a lesson. I knew about Trout; they had spots. We borrowed a couple of fiberglass flyrods and some flies from a friend of my Dad's. "The boy know how to use them?" he asked my Dad, who replied, "He's had some experience." I was glad he hadn't quoted the story in full as I'm telling it to you.

The friend of my Dad held out his fly box and said, "Pick what you want."

"Well," said I, eyeing the treasures and growing confused, "well, well, well." I reached out and latched onto the largest and gaudiest fly in the box. "Well . . .," I repeated again a couple of times as I assumed what I felt was my most knowledgeable stance; I held the fly out and squinted! "Looks pretty good," said I. "I'll use this."

"I decorated already
beautiful trees with my fly!"

"Mickey Finn," murmured my father.

"Yes, Mickey Finn," said I like an echo!

"Should be good," said the friend. "The water is high."

"Yes sir," I thought to myself, but what is it?

"They'll go for a minnow imitation," said Dad, reading my thoughts.

"Ah, yes, I should think so." I smiled, knowing now that I knew what I knew, and soon would be teaching my Dad how to take Trout. Although I confess his next statement surprised me. I was beginning to wonder just exactly how little he knew.

"I think I'll stick to an Iron Blue Dun or an Atherton six," he said as he reached for the box. I assumed that he must have read quite a bit.

"An Iron Blue six should be just about right," I spoke up with authority, confirming his choice and assuring his confidence right from the start.

Down by the river what a contrast I found to my lily pad–slow-running rivers of home; here was the coolest and most beautiful world I'd yet found. Here the river gurgled and sang as it rushed past the birch and the alders and flowering dogwood and wild mountain laurel. I think I was quite unprepared for the sight—for the look and the feel. I know now looking back that I certainly was unprepared for the flyrod. I kind of stalled for awhile, allowing my Dad the first cast. To be perfectly honest, I had no idea how it worked, but I reasoned I could help my Dad more by watching and commenting on his form. I was quite pleased to realize in a moment that I wasn't going to have to drive him too hard with a lesson on casting. He shook his line out and then back—his rod high in the air—the line gathered its speed and shot forward, seeming to float to the water forty feet out. I watched with approval as he shot a couple more. Completely satisfied with his progress, I shouted encouragement. "Get a big one!"

Then I moved on down river to perfect my own amazing technique, which, to a casual observer, might have seemed quite a mess at first, though really it wasn't. I just unfortunately had hooked myself in the shoulder on the very first cast, which naturally threw me off stride as it would indeed have thrown anyone. After a while, though, I had it under control. I also practiced a few common faults, like decorating already beautiful trees with my Mickey Finn. This I did with the hopes of becoming an even better teacher. After all, one must experience a few mistakes in order to correct them in others. Later, at a pool near a small waterfall, I got down to business and flicked out a pretty fair cast, not much for distance but all in all a pretty fair cast. The flow of the river grabbed at my lure and swung it around in a sweep toward the falls, when the fish hit—I had seen his mad rush, the flash when he hit, and his beauty when he took to the air! He wasn't a very large fish, and I suppose that I had him to net in a minute or two. I had been surprised by his strength and thrilled by his beauty—a Brook Trout, a colorful Char—who was for me at that time and is still for me now the most beautiful fish in the world. Of course, as you know, the point of the story is that Dad managed a couple of fish for himself on that day. And why not? After all, it was I who had had faith in his use of the Atherton six or the Iron Blue Dun.

Salmon

There would be no way to write a handbook for teachers of fishing without including a chapter on Salmon.

There are SALMON on both coasts of our country. On the Pacific Coast, we have a number of species, while on the Atlantic Coast there is only *one*. Now, tell Dad not to go feeling sorry for the Atlantic Ocean, for in this case the one that they have, the Atlantic Salmon, *Salmo Salar,* is far and away quite the best. (If he must feel sorry for anyone, tell him to feel for the West.)

By tradition (like eating dessert), we shall save the best for the last. Let's start Dad off with his lesson by explaining just who the Salmon are that live in the West.

The CHINOOK (his scientific name *Oncorhynchus tshawytscha* suggests that he is a big guy indeed, and he is): In a case like this you might call out to Dad if you are lucky enough to catch one: "Hey! Dad, I've got an oversized Oncorhynchus." Or you might try one of the other names that he goes by, like KING SALMON or SPRING SALMON. At any rate, Mr. Chinook is by quite a bit the largest of the Salmon. He is known to reach a weight of better than 126 pounds. He lives in the Pacific Northwest (as do all of the Pacific Salmon) from northern California on up into Alaska. Although the Chinook can be and is caught by sportsmen on lures—large spoons and plugs—he is most often taken on rigged baits, trolled deep off the mouths of rivers that he enters to spawn. At this point we won't elaborate on the technique for taking this fish. Later, perhaps, in the story of fishing for Salmon there might be a few hints.

The CHUM SALMON (*Oncorhynchus keta*) is a medium-sized fish that reaches a weight of perhaps thirty pounds; the average weight taken by fishermen runs to about ten pounds. Chum's range is about the same as the Chinook's.

The COHO or SILVER SALMON (*Oncorhynchus kisutch*) runs about the same size as the Chum Salmon. If I were out after a Pacific Salmon this is the guy that I'd want. He readily takes flies and for sure a variety of spinning type lures; he's a great jumper when hooked and for that reason alone he'd be my choice for "the best of the West!" You would have to check locally for the best times of the year to fish for Mr. Coho, for his run varies quite greatly from river to river.

The PINK SALMON (*Oncorhynchus gorbuscha*) is the smallest member of the Pacific Salmons. He averages less than five pounds and rarely goes as heavy as ten. He is sometimes called the "Little Chinook," which, of course, he is not.

The SOCKEYE SALMON (*Oncorhynchus nerka*) is in many ways a bit of a nerk, as his name suggests. He's the guy who most often winds up in cans. Excellent! He's delicious! He rarely takes lures and when rarely he does (at least in Canada) he's not legal and must be released. On the bright side for fishermen, however, is that the Sockeye sometimes chooses to live his life as a nonmigratory form: when he has made this choice then he is called KOKANEE. He hangs around the larger lakes out in the West and definitely will take the lure. He is delicious to eat fresh from the lake, a lot better than canned.

Now that we've learned who lives in the West, let's cross the country for our dessert.

The ATLANTIC SALMON (*Salmo salar*) is the best and most magnificent freshwater fish of them all. Salmo Salar is the top of the line of the Salmonidae family of fishes, which includes all of the Trout and Pacific Salmon as well. Because Mr. Salmo Salar is so very special, I think that you should treat him as a legend and depart from your usual lesson on how to catch fish. When you are finished, I think, Dad will quite understand and maybe applaud all your efforts. What you will teach is a lot about love and a lot about dreams, for that is what this fish represents. Know right from the start that not everybody has the chance just to go out and take Mr. Salar. Some day, if you fall in love with the fishermen's world and are lucky, you might, but, even if not, you and your Dad will still be among the luckiest fishermen just in knowing this fish. Let's explain to your Dad just who Salmo Salar is, where he lives, and some of the interesting known and unknown aspects of his life.

The ATLANTIC SALMON is a fish of the Northern Atlantic Ocean, living as far north as Greenland (look at a map). Here in our country he is found as far south as a few rivers in Maine. In the old days, when our country was first settled, this Salmon was plentiful even in New York's Hudson River. He is smarter perhaps than we are, because when the rivers turned sour and ran with the filth of the land, Mr. Salmon departed. I'm sure that if he could have done anything about it he never would have allowed it to happen. Maybe someday we (you and your Dad) may change things around—clean it up—ask Mr. Salmon to come back again. I'm sure he would if we could keep our part of the bargain. He is found also in Europe, up where it's cold (think of Norway). It is here in Norwegian rivers that the Atlantic Salmon reaches its greatest size, which is known to be at least 100 pounds. (Help us all if you were ever able to hook one that big.) The world's record to date on rod and reel came from a river in Norway and weighed 79½ pounds.

With no exceptions, all Salmon are born in freshwater, then—with only two exceptions—migrate down to the sea. The exceptions to migrating are the Kokanee, which we have discussed, and a form of the Atlantic Salmon who was landlocked many thousands of years ago—when the glaciers of the Ice Age receded. He is called the LANDLOCKED SALMON. He has no outlet to the ocean; he lives in lake waters, principally in the state of Maine, though he has been transported to and stocked in other places where water conditions are to his liking. New Hampshire and New York have some populations of Landlocks. One of the best places to find them now is in Argentina. Landlocks generally run smaller than the big sea-run Atlantics. The largest Landlock to date (as far as I know) is 36 pounds, and he was not taken by rod, but rather by biologists with a net up in Sebago Lake, Maine.

But let's take some time and tell Dad all about the life of a Salmon, one of the ones that run to the sea.

Forget for a moment the riddle: "Which came first, the Salmon or the egg?" Let's start with the egg and be thankful that as long as one or the other came first at least they are here. It is fall. Somewhere up a wild, clear, and cold-running stream, many miles from the ocean, a Salmon egg hatches in a nest called a "redd." What has hatched, of course, looks nothing at all like a Salmon, not even half as much as a newly hatched chick looks like a chicken. I would guess that the best way to describe the new little salmon would be to say, "Hey, a transparent worm!" and you would add, as you puzzled over it, "with some sort of sac or bubble attached up near its head. At least, I guess it's a head."

Well, explain to your Dad that what's attached is a yolk sac, which will nourish the young Salmon for a short while. The Salmon is called an *alevin* at this stage of his life. He is one of perhaps a few thousand eggs that the female had deposited in the redd. Not many survive, for the eggs fall prey to all sorts of egg lovers: other fish, minnows, and insects, not to mention those eggs that unhappily get washed away in a flood or whatever.

But this one survives, and soon he grows into a small silvery fish like a minnow. He develops a few red and black spots (almost dots), and then larger blotches (called *parr markings*) appear on his sides. At this point give him a new name to swim around with: he is now called a *parr*, in honor of his dark blotches. When he loses his parr markings and turns silver, he has been swimming his stream and his river for a couple of years and has grown to and is now known as a *smolt.* This isn't a bad name at all for a fish that started out life as an alevin. Personally I'm not so sure I'd be crazy about either.

As a smolt, he's a young fellow and ripe for adventure. After all, he would reason, he's been hanging around the same old river for two or three years (some even stick around for a full four). At any rate, it's time to head for the sea, where he will grow at a considerable rate. Most Salmon spend three winters at sea, a few will be gone for as many as six, and then there are some smart little smolts that return to the river after only one winter and again get a new name. These four-pounders are called *grilse.* Never you mind, next year they'll be back to the sea and grow up into Salmon, which is the best name of all. I think it time for you to tell Dad a mysterious and interesting fact:

All Salmon that run out to sea always return, when they are ready to spawn, to the *very same* rivers and streams where they were born. And it doesn't matter how long they've been gone or how far, which in most cases can be thousands of miles and, as you now know, up to six years. No one knows how they do it (after all there are hundreds and hundreds of rivers and thousands of streams feeding into the ocean), but do it they do. Some scientists speak of landmarks and contours; others think perhaps it has to do with differences of the saltiness or the chemical makeup of rivers (no two would be exactly alike). Well, perhaps it's part of all of these things and perhaps again it's currents and channels and temperatures that hide in the sea and can be known and understood only by Salmon. Perhaps, it's innate timing and compass instincts that we'll never know. Nature at her most magnificent best has over eons built natural timeclocks and computers in Salmon that are in tune with the currents of Earth and the subtle pressures exerted by the contact of worlds out in space. After all we use the stars for our most complex navigational feats. Anyway, Atlantic Salmon from Europe and America share the same feeding grounds in the waters near Greenland, and how they get home without translators and tour guides is one of the greatest of mysteries.

Now I have to tell you a very sad thing about our Pacific Coast Salmon, but Nature planned it that way, so it works.

All Pacific Salmon die after spawning, after beating their way sometimes as much as two thousand miles up rivers and streams just to get home where they started. The Salmon spawn and then die. It's a sad sight after watching them struggle so hard up the rapids and falls. It is awesome and wonderful too. I wish that everyone could see it and understand.

The Atlantic Salmon is the exception. He struggles as hard to get home, but after spawning some will return to the sea, repeating the cycle a number of times. I think, for this reason, for the celebration of life, that many experienced Atlantic Salmon fishermen will release their catch after enjoying the mangificent fight of landing them.

Look at the illustrations of Salmon on page 59.

SALMON • 57

A Story About Salmon

Not many of us have a chance to collect a great many stories about Salmon. For most of us it's a once-in-a-lifetime trip, which is okay when you think how much richer your life has been made. Of course, please understand that I am not speaking of deep trolling off Oregon's coast with rigged herring bait. This is one kind of fishing with its own kind of thrills, but the fishing I mean is the wilderness kind with a flyrod and a moment or two when you get as close to heaven as you can on this earth. I never understood this when I was young. A good hunk of my life had already passed when I first met *Salmo salar,* which as far as I can see, looking back, is the only penalty one suffers growing up in Florida.

There are other penalties in life that having nothing to do with growing up in Florida or late starts in the pursuit of Salmon. The loss of my star pupil was the greatest of these; he had hung up his rod long before I first met the Salmon. I like to think, with his love of clean and beautiful rivers, that long before I entered his life and assumed the role of his teacher he himself had done his share of the teaching up on some river deep in the wilds of Quebec.

Perhaps it might bother you to hear a fisherman talk bluntly about losses and gains in this life. Well, don't let it bother you too much. Just file it away under "things that must be" and think of the Salmon, his stages in life and his struggles, and you'll realize that fish and fisherman share many traits.

You might say that I had a surrogate father when I first met a Salmon. I was with a man that I loved and respected. His name was Joe Brooks. He too has now hung up his rod, but only after he'd created a marvelous world for all fishermen through his books and his knowledge and love of the sport. I was producing and writing a show for ABC-TV called "The American Sportsman," a wonderful show that featured the world's finest fishermen, Mr. Lee Wulff, Mr. "Grits" Gresham, and, last and most important to me, Mr. Brooks. He walked into my office one day; it was the first time we'd met, as I was new on the job.

"Hi! Like to go fishing?" he asked.

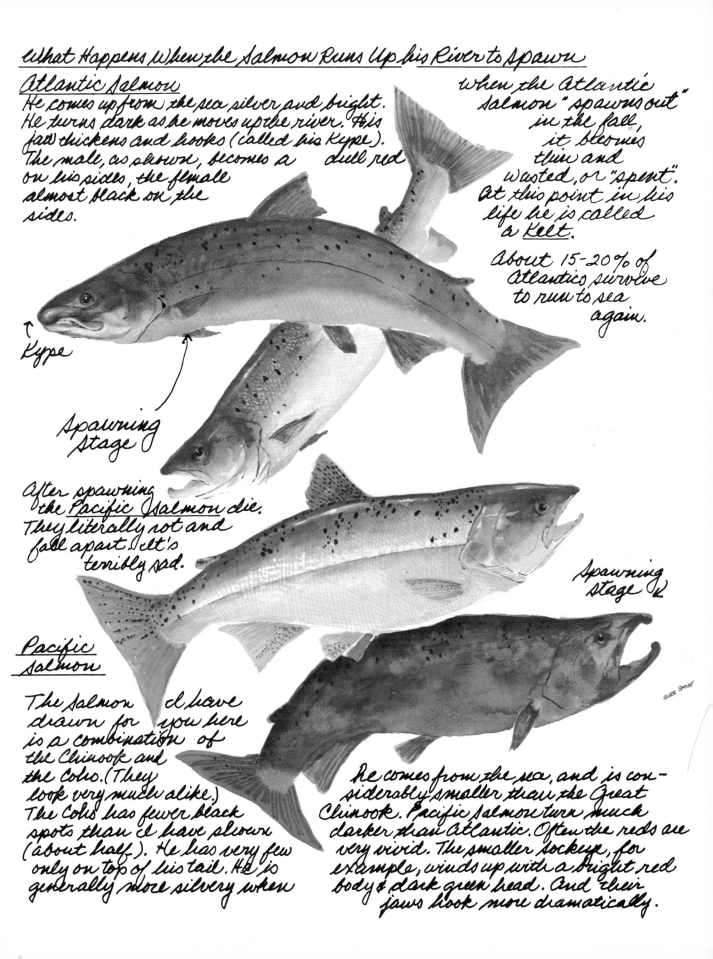

What Happens When the Salmon Runs Up his River to Spawn

Atlantic Salmon

He comes up from the sea silver and bright. He turns dark as he moves up the river. His jaw thickens and hooks (called his Kype). The male, as shown, becomes a dull red on his sides, the female almost black on the sides.

Kype

Spawning Stage

When the Atlantic Salmon "spawns out" in the fall, it becomes thin and wasted, or "spent". At this point in his life he is called a Kelt.

About 15-20% of Atlantics survive to run to sea again.

After spawning the Pacific Salmon die. They literally rot and fall apart. It's terribly sad.

Spawning stage

Pacific Salmon

The Salmon I have drawn for you here is a combination of the Chinook and the Coho. (They look very much alike.) The Coho has fewer black spots than I have shown (about half). He has very few only on top of his tail. He is generally more silvery when he comes from the sea, and is considerably smaller than the Great Chinook. Pacific Salmon turn much darker than Atlantic. Often the reds are very vivid. The smaller sockeye, for example, winds up with a bright red body & dark green head. And their jaws hook more dramatically.

The Terrible Pikes

Muskellunge

Northern Pike

Grass Pickerel

Chain Pickerel

Redfin Pickerel

BURR SMIDT

He walked through a Revolution and hardly noticed it!

And, I, like the new producer I was, mumbled, "Yes." I guess in a way I wasn't as dumb as I thought at the time, for I quickly realized that nobody, but nobody (who was sane), would say "No" to a chance to go fishing with Mr. Joe Brooks. I must confess, now looking back, that the next few days were a nightmare. It was a *must go at once* hurry-up trip to the Rio Traful for *Salmo salar* of the Landlocked tribe; they were running *just then*. I mean NOW!

"The Rio Traful?" I asked, thinking perhaps that it was in some part of Maine I hadn't heard of.

"You'll love the West Argentine!" he replied.

And I did.

The nightmare, of course, was getting everything ready in too short a time. The cameras and crew, the passports and visas and "shots" and the "star," in this case a wonderful actor, Mr. David

Wayne, who loved fishing every bit as much as did I. Well, we got there (and don't ask me how). There was a revolution going full steam ahead when we arrived—fortunately fishermen hardly notice such things (if they happen on the way to the sport). Anyway, we cut through red tape and machine guns, talking of nothing but Salmon the while, and twenty air hours later, and a few by jeep, we arrived at the Rio Traful, a short walk down from the lake of the same last name. All I can say is "What a beautiful spot to meet your first *Salmo salar*": in the background the rise of the Andes; at our feet beautiful pools of clean and cold water, the pool Leonora and another called Pool of Plenty. There we would fish.

We stayed at a beautiful Argentine ranch, named for the Lady of Spring, "La Primavera," owned by the most gracious of hosts, Felipe Lariviere. As I said, Salmon fishing can be a once-in-a-lifetime kind of trip.

Next morning we set up the camera. We were all quite excited, for down in the Pool of Plenty we saw a number of Salmon at rest. It looked as if it would be the easiest show in the world to record (although, believe me, none of them are). Fish have an acting technique all their own, more complicated even than Marlon Brando's. They just wouldn't play for the cameras. For three days we fished and we tried. It looked like we'd have a grand travelogue for the Rio Traful—but no fish. "I don't understand them," said Joe. "I think we should try a Honey Blonde." I agreed.

I've got to tell you just how frustrating all of this was, me being a new and untried producer and all, thousands of American Broadcasting Company's dollars bet on a fish. And by far the worst of it all, I, as producer, wasn't allowed to fish. "There's too much danger that you'll disturb the beautiful pool" . . . and I agreed through my tears. After all, I had waited so long for Salmo Salar, I could now only envision crossing back through the battle lines of Buenos Aires with empty creel and shattered hopes. I was considering perhaps joining up—either one side or the other (anything at that moment was preferable to a trip back to New York with no film). I could hear it all: "Yes, that was our producer! But he flunked on a fish." My mind wandered out through the Andes with all sorts of horrible thoughts that clashed with the beauty . . . and then came a *YELL!*

"Fish on!"

David had made a beautiful cast with his Honey Blonde and the cameras were rolling. I had never seen such acrobatics—really such grandeur—as the Salmon came up with a twisting great leap and a flip, flashing his great silver body. He ran down toward the tail of the pool, smoking the reel, then turned for an unbelievable dash straight up the river. In ten minutes or so David had his fish tailed, near the shore. After the picture of David's great smile and a few shots of twelve pounds of beautiful fish, we let him go (the Salmon, of course).

It was then that I came to love Joe Brooks . . . "It's over," he said. "Here, take my rod and go catch a fish. I've been watching your face for a couple of days . . . and I know how it hurts." Then he explained that this was the way with the Salmon: he'll take when he wants to, and sometimes you can wait for a week, advice that to me was horribly sad; it was over. We were scheduled to leave when the day drew to a close. "I knew he'd go for the Honey Blonde; now stick to it, work it across and down to the tail of the pool," he said with a smile and added, "You'll do it . . . tight lines . . ."

Then he turned and started up the bank while I stepped out into the stream. I gave a couple of casts, hoping with all my heart (against hope). Then I spied Joe. He hadn't deserted, but was sitting comfortable and cool beneath a tree high on the bank, watching me—and he winked. I threw one more cast—my best of the few that I'd taken—all I heard was "Tight lines" when the fish took. I held him for fair a minute or two, then he came high and handsome straight for the sky twisting and turning like a small Tarpon (of which, being from Florida, I'd caught quite a few) but at the moment I knew that I was into the fish of all fish as he came back to the water and started a dash that in ignorance I thought I could stop. And he was gone. I felt that I had tried to tame lightning, but in the trying I knew that I could walk the rest of my life through the battles and know that there are "things that must be." Most important—all important—"tight lines," as Joe had wished it to me.

The Pike
And His Family

If the story I told you about the Black Bass eating ducklings (with or without applesauce) was a bit chilling to you, well, hold on to your waders, you are about to meet someone who will give you the sweats and then freeze you in ice.

In introducing the PIKE I shall tell you in passing that there are in our country five members of this most "terrible" tribe. They belong to the family of fishes called Esocidae, or *Esox* for short. "Hey! Dad, I've hooked an *Esox!*" Try saying that quietly when indeed you have hooked one and you'll find that you can't. It will come out in a scream heard clear 'round the lake. They are BIG. Perhaps I should say that the top two members of this tribe are the Muskellunge and the Northern Pike.

The Muskellunge (*Esox masquinongy*), just call him "Muskie" as everyone does, is the biggest and is known to reach at least one hundred pounds. Of course, don't count on taking one of this size, for I'm sure that you won't; but if you did I'm just as sure that your shout "I've got a *really big ole Esox*" would blow you apart. Fifteen to twenty pounders are more common. The second in terms of his size, up to twenty-plus pounds, is the "great" NORTHERN PIKE (*Exos lucius*) or the "Pitiless Pike" named, because of the shape of his head, for the weapon of medieval times, the combination of the axe and the spear, ergo the Pike. Perhaps at this point you might be getting the point that these are really tough fish. Uh-huh . . . you are right!

Try and stay calm and describe them to Dad.

They are long and lean fish. Think of a four-foot banana that's green, with some splotches and blotches and bars. Add some fins and a mouth shaped like a duck's bill. Then fill the mouth with teeth, lots of teeth, in fact add a few more and make sure that they

I've done color pictures of these mean old guys for you on page 92.

are long and horribly sharp; put some (a lot) on the roof of his mouth, and then curve them back so you'll know that whatever he bites he'll never let go. By now, if you've told him just right (let your eyes bug out a bit when you talk), Dad should know what a Muskie or Pike looks like. (If not, show him the picture.) Don't let your Dad get the idea at this point that he should be afraid to go and catch PIKE, for he shouldn't (just have him prepared for the thrill). Explain that his reputation (the PIKE's) for fierceness only extends to the creatures that live in his lake, like the poor little duckling who seems to get caught in all sorts of plots. Actually, the PIKE's food is other fish that are smaller than he. I guess, sad to say, that would be most other fish that live in his lake, like Perch or Trout, Ciscos and Suckers, Whitefish and Minnows of various types, Sunfish and Basses, Bluegills and Crappies and, too, Pikes that are smaller. I suppose, now that you've seen who he eats, it might be fair to call him an opportunistic-type feeder (don't be alarmed: he never eats people, even if given the opportunity).

Now that you and your Dad have met Mr. Pike and naturally fallen in love with him, tell your Dad where he lives.

The Northern Pike has a wider range than the Muskie and is commoner in the range they both share. I expect that he is the one that most of us will meet when we first start out fishing for Pike. His natural range in our country is central and western New York state through western Pennsylvania, all through the area of the Great Lakes and those states that border them, west into parts of Missouri, Iowa, and eastern Nebraska. His greatest concentration is northern New York up through the Great Lakes and into the part of Canada adjacent to that area. Pike are found somewhat spottily all across Canada's West into the eastern part of British Columbia, and there only in a very few rivers that drain to the east. I'm not sure, but I've heard it reported that they are also found in northern Alaska in a few drainage systems that reach the Arctic Ocean. The Northern Pike has been introduced to a wider area in the United States than his natural range suggests . . . into New England, and, in particular, the Connecticut River system. He has been introduced in the South, at least as far south as North Carolina. I would doubt though that the quality of fishing would approach what is found in the Pike's natural range.

The Muskie is rather limited even in sections that make up his home. He is a U.S.-Canadian border-type citizen, the St. Lawrence system through the Great Lakes and down into parts of the Ohio River drainage. He is found in limited areas of western New York and Pennsylvania and down into Tennessee. His range is constantly being expanded, so you might ask about and look for him in all the areas I've mentioned, any place where the water in the rivers runs slow and is cool, or in clean, cold-water lakes that have an abundance of grass and lily-pad growth. If you can't raise a Muskie in

There are some pictures of a few of his favorite foods on the next page.

Food fish of the Pike

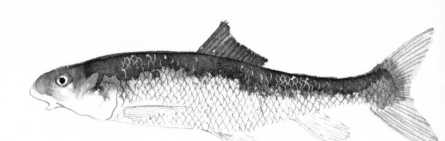

Typical Sucker

These old "duddies" are nobody's favorite. But I don't mind them at all. I just think of all my fish friends that they feed.

Typical Cisco

This guy, one of the favorite foods of the big Bass and the Pikes, is related (at least distantly) to the salmon and Trout. At times they are rather fine "gamefish" themselves, and take flies and spinners. There are a number of species that are known to reach a weight of six or seven pounds.

Typical Minnow

The true minnows belong to the very large family Cyprinidae (about 2000 species, world wide). There are 200 species in North America. Although they are almost exclusively fresh water fish; the Dace, Shiners and Chubs, fishermen refer to most small, schooling baitfish, fresh or saltwater, as minnows.

Most are quite small, but a few, like the Carp, grow to a very large size

Typical Whitefish

Related to Mr. Cisco, above. Both the lake whitefish and the mountain whitefish are fine gamesters on flyrods — as well as helping us out by being food for the lake Trout and Pikes, not to mention ourselves.

66

water like that, at least the chances are good that you'll meet and catch one of the other Pike members.

The easiest way to tell Northern Pike and Muskie apart is by coloration and markings. Any large Pike that has light spots that are slightly oblong or oval would undoubtedly be a Northern, while any larger Pike with bars on his sides or spots that are darker than the background color would probably be Muskie. Other members of the Pike family that you are very likely to meet are the Pickerels: the GRASS PICKEREL, the REDFIN, and the EASTERN CHAIN PICKEREL, this latter being quite the largest of the three, a two or three pounder's a good one (it is rumored that they run up to eight). If I caught one that big, I'd certainly check for those light spots that are common to the Northern. Pickerel have a much wider range than their big brothers; you will find them all through the East, through the entire range of the Muskie and Pike, in the South and the Midwest. Look for them in slow-running rivers, in lakes and ponds that have an abundance of grass. Generally you will catch one when you are fishing for somebody else like a Bass or even a Trout. They are fun on very light tackle, and I suggest that after he's jumped and done all his tricks let him go, which advice you might pass on to Dad as regards all of the Pike. They are a fine and wonderful sportfish, but they do not distinguish themselves on the table. Some may dispute me on that, but, believe me, this fish-loving chef doesn't enjoy (after the fun) going home and fighting with thousands of bones.

As to tackle for Pike, tell Dad that the light little outfit that he might use for Trout or Pickerel is hardly suited for Northern and Muskies. These big, heavy fish wouldn't even know they were hooked on such a fine little toy. Tell Dad when fishing in waters that hold the big Pike to go to a freshwater, medium-class rod or light heavy-duty that handles an eight- to ten-pound test line and lures from $5/8$ ounce to 1 ounce in weight. If Dad is courageous, he'll have more fun with the lighter of these.

There is a wide range of lures that take Pike (you might have guessed that from their diet). You will never go wrong if you stick to your Rapalas and Mepps—in larger sizes, of course—like Rapala plugs in 13 magnum size, silver or gold, or the Mepps Comets with blades number five. As all of the Pikes feed in reasonably shallow water (except for the hottest of months) down to a depth of no more than fifteen or so feet (usually much shallower than that), surface-type lures are often quite good, Poppers and Chuggers and Swimmers. Also large flashing Spoons are always very good; try for example the Red Eye Wiggler or the Dardevle, red and white $2\frac{1}{2}$ to 3 inches in size.

One of the cautions (you must advise Dad) is to be careful in boating and landing big Pike (remember those teeth). Always, if you wish to release your fish, use a deep-bag large landing net. Release the hook with a pair of long-nosed pliers (the longer the better). If you intend keeping a fish for a trophy, *use a gaff,* and really make sure that he's completely subdued and under control before you hoist him aboard. *Watch out for your hands and your feet and everything else* or you'll have a PIKE story that's painful to tell.

A HINT: When retrieving your lure while fishing for Pike, reel fairly fast, much faster than you did for the Trout and the Bass. The big Pike can't seem to stand even the thought that something that looks good to eat might get away.

Afternoons in the early fall months are the best times for MUSKIES, while mornings when the sun is up are best for the Northern Pike. Both fish seem to be primarily daytime feeders; feeding seems to fall off in the evening. The Northern Pike is far more reliable than the Muskie and is taken from spring right through fall. Of course, when the water is cooler I think that the fishing is best. If for no other reason they'll be close to the shallows and weed beds.

A Story About Pike

Back in the good old days when I was eight, maybe nine, and learning all about fish (that's why I call it the good old days, since any day you learn about fish is technically a good old day), I guess I was excited or maybe even mad—I don't know—I could have been either. Anyway, if I was excited, it was because my Dad had announced that we were taking a trip to the north, all the way to New York. If I was mad, it was simply because everyone, at least everyone that I knew, knew for a certain that good fishing stopped with a screech right at the county line in Florida where I lived. And believe me, we knew that it didn't make a worm can full of difference which direction you took, except possibly west, where the county line stretched on into the Gulf and as far as was known all the way to Mexico, so, in fact, we could reason with a certain certitude that the west end of the line was the only possible exception.

New York, of course, as even I knew, was at some considerable distance north of my country's boundary. My Dad was still in the midst of being taught the facts about fishing by none other than myself, so who better than I to know that he knew nothing about boundaries at all? I could only scoff lightly as he stuffed a couple of baitcasting rods on the roof of the car.

The reason I scoffed lightly was that that was far better than to take the time to explain, for I knew just how discouraged he'd be if he knew. He'd have to find out for himself, and sometimes that's the best form of teaching. I contented myself with dropping a hint as we passed under the arches of the north county line: "Bet there won't be no fish north of here!" Well, he smiled, so I guess I hadn't done too much discouraging damage.

I won't bore you with the details of the trip, simply say that they were just building that Route Number 1 and there wasn't a bridge all the way from my home till we got to Virginia. We had to ferry all the streams, rivers, and creeks by cable-pulled barges and the road wasn't paved most of the way either, just a bed of crushed rock that played on your nerves—mine in particular—knowing that there'd be no fish at the end of the line.

We poked around New York City for I guess like a week, and if it hadn't been for the trucks that were driven by chains and rode on solid rubber tires I would have got really real bored in a town with no fish.

It was my Dad who finally saved me, as he usually did. "How would you like to take a trip to a lake that I know way up near the top of this state?" he said. Well, I was certainly game and I said so. I knew that I could give him some good casting lessons; I knew there wouldn't be fish.

The lake was quite pretty, though not very big, I guess no more than a mile and a half at the longest and about three quarters of a

I was sad. Everyone knew there were no fish north of the county line!

mile wide. It looked deep except near the edges and down at one end where there was a profusion of lily pads growing and the bottom you could easily see was covered with waving weeds.

Dad had hired an old boat with an outboard motor, an old Evinrude, that smoked and sputtered, making more noise than the trucks of the city. But it ran. My Dad pulled out a couple of brass spoons that were as big as any I'd seen and said we'd troll. Well, now, that was no way to teach casting, but I readily agreed. It was too early to get him discouraged with knowledge. The spoons were too big, but no matter; I wasn't about to let on all that I knew. We went trolling close to the weed patch at a pretty good clip. I knew it wouldn't be of much use. It was time I took over. "Out there!" I pointed. "Out where it's deep!"

I never added more of my wisdom for, at precisely that moment, I caught what I thought was the bottom. I thought so at least until the bottom started running as strong as a cable-pulled barge. The reel handle cracked all my knuckles and the spool of the reel spun with a blur and put a burn on my thumb that took off the prints. I swear I don't swear to this day; I don't swear. But I swear that I swore at that moment. I guess my Dad was laughing so hard he never heard what I said. But once again I swear and, believe me, whatever I'd said was nothing to what I thought when we got that fish up to the boat. It was as big as myself and looked mean. It was then that it shook its powerful head and I caught sight of the teeth. I sweated and turned into ice, which became quite a habit that day.

Now I don't know about you, but I sure know about me, and whenever something mean comes along and gives me a scare I tend to overreact. In this case, I just wanted to catch more and more of these fish. It's sort of like the thrill you get from a roller coaster ride, when you pretend you are brave and want to go back. Of course, I know now, looking back, that I did myself irreparable damage: every time I go to New York I get scared.

Freshwater Fun Fish

There is quite a mixed tribe of small fighting fish in the ponds, rivers, and lakes all over our country. I used to think that they belonged exclusively to barefoot boys, willow poles, and bent pins, but now that I've been through all of that and ripened a bit I can look back and realize that perhaps I was playing Tom Sawyer and trying to keep a good thing to myself.

Believe me, if you feel even a little that way, well, don't! Let poor old Dad in on the fun. You'll never regret or forget your good deed and neither will he. (Think of your birthday and Christmas.)

Show Dad the pictures of these small scrappy guys, and then sit down and figure where close to home you can run out to catch them. Of course, at least one of them is not really small, and that is the Walleye, so I think we should start off with him.

The WALLEYE (*Stizostedion vitreum vitreum*): Now there is one scientific name I'd hate to call out. Imagine: "Father dear, I seem to have engaged a *Stizostedion vitreum vitreum* in battle." Say this quite calmly and then scream for *HELP!* The Walleye, the largest of the freshwater Perches, has been known to reach twenty pounds. Figure however that the average might be closer to three or four pounds. Any Walleye over five or six pounds would be considered a prize.

The Walleye and the Sauger look so much alike that I've drawn only a picture of a Walleye. You can tell them apart by the white tip on the tail (that I've circled). The Walleye has one, the Sauger doesn't!

In some localities the Walleye is called, incorrectly, a Pike, like, for example, "Walleyed Pike," "Jack Pike," or, worse yet, just plain old "Pike." He is not related to old *Esox* at all; he is now and forever a Perch.

The Walleye likes rather large bodies of clear and deep water. Any deep spot by the dam in a river or lake that is clear and on the cool side, with a gravelly bottom and with cover nearby, is a good place to look for him. His range was originally the northeastern parts of the country, up into Canada. Because he's such a popular guy, he has been transplanted all over the place in many lakes of the West and the South.

He's a hard-hitting fish that loves any lure that looks like a Minnow for dinner. Try the small plugs and the spinners. The Walleye has one very close relative that is also found in much the same range, and that is the SAUGER (*Stizostedion canadense*) and, though as a rule he runs considerably smaller than the Walleye, perhaps reaching a weight of close to eight pounds as a limit, he nevertheless likes only *really large* lakes. Fish both species alike, rather deep in the lake.

A WHOLE FAMILY OF SUNFISH AND CRAPPIES (excluding the Basses, whom you've already met):

Here is a grouping of fish that contains a large number of species (certainly more than thirty in our country alone). Because most look alike and have very similar habits, we'll try to treat them as one grand experience. Besides, I guarantee you that you'd go sunfishy yourself if you tried to keep them in order.

Here are five pictures of most common species, just so you can see what I mean.

The BLACK CRAPPIE
(*Pomoxis nigromaculatus*)

Black Crappie
He is very closely related to the White Crappie, who has vertical bars on his side so that you can tell them apart.

The BLUEGILL (*Lepomis machrochirus*)

Bluegill
He is easily
identified by
the blue color
and patch on
his gill
(Operculum).

The GREEN SUNFISH (*Lepomis cyanellus*)

Green Sunfish
An overall greenish
color and a
small touch of red
behind the dark
spot on his oper-
culum introduces
the Green Sunfish.
He loves small
lures and flies
and is one
of the more
willing battlers
of the sunfish
family.

FRESHWATER
74 • FUN FISH

The REDEAR SUNFISH
(*Lepomis microlophus*)

Redear Sunfish
This guy has a very definite spot of color on the tip of his gill flap, behind the typical dark splotch. It is red on the males and quite orange on the ladies. Down in Georgia and Florida some people call him "Stumpknocker". Incidentally, he has a northern cousin, the War mouth, who is also called the "stump-knocker".

The SACRAMENTO PERCH (*Archoplites interruptus*):

This is the only member of the Sunfish family that is native west of the Rockies (he was originally found in the Sacramento and San Joaquin river systems, but has since been introduced into parts of Nevada and Utah). One of the largest of the Sunfishes, he is known to reach a weight of nearly ten pounds.

Now! One or more species of these fine little fish will be found in almost any body of water you happen upon. I would think that most of the farm ponds of the nation have some, as do the lakes and the ponds of the parks in most citites; lakes, rivers, and ditches (that maintain enough water year round), all are good possibilities. I would guess that, except for those who live in the heart of Death Valley, no one has to move very far to have a great deal of fun. All Sunfish that I know of can be taken on lures, small little spinners or micro-type jigs. They will also rush either a wet or dry fly and give you a fit. Most of the fish in this group will run less than a pound; but don't be deceived, for if you use ultra light tackle you will have your hands full. And believe me, if a Crappie or Bluegill comes along that weighs as much as four or five pounds, you're the one they'll be calling a Walleye.

The WHITE BASS (*Morone chrysops*) and the YELLOW BASS (*Morone mississippienis*) and their crazy old cousin, the WHITE PERCH (*Morone americana*), who can't seem to make up his mind as to what flavor of water he prefers, all share a few things in common. They school, are voracious feeders, are easy to take on any numbers and types of lures, are strong fighters and great fish on the fly rod, and are delicious eating.

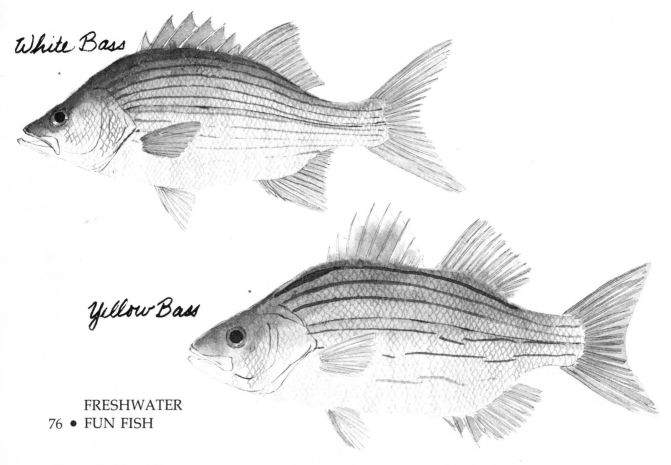

White Bass

Yellow Bass

FRESHWATER
76 • FUN FISH

White Perch

The out-of-step guy (if there's any) is the Perch. He can tolerate and live in brackish water, salt or fresh. His range is the eastern seaboard from eastern Canada down to the Carolinas. These fish seem to prefer freshwater ponds that have some outlet to the sea. They have been spreading westward of recent years, as far as the Great Lakes; I would suppose that some of the inland seaways are responsible.

They are an ideal little fish on the fly rod; in summer, come evening, they rise to the insect hatches much as the Trout do. They are prolific and sometimes the schools are quite large. You can have literally hours of fun without moving too far from a favorite spot. Incidentally, they are in my opinion one of the finest panfish of all for the table: roll the filets in corn meal and fry them.

The White and Yellow Bass are fish of similar habits and waters. The White has a chance to meet more fishermen because his range is considerably broader. But no matter, for if you live in the East, or in the central parts of the country, near the Mississippi or Missouri river drainages, or in parts of the South and Southwest, you'll eventually meet one or the other. Look for them in the larger lakes and reservoirs; evening is the best time of the day for you to put on a smile and go out and make their acquaintance, for this is the time that they move in from deep water to the shallows for feeding. Often, you can spot the large and dense schools as they feed at the surface; what was once a glassy, smooth lake is whipped into foam as they chase small Minnows about (varieties of small Smelt or Shad). These Bass certainly know how to disturb the peace of the land as well as the mind of the fisherman. Use very light tackle and the smallest of lures, little spinners, plugs, and spoons, not to mention your fly rod and imitations of bugs.

The White Bass, like the White Perch, is an excellent fish to have over for dinner, so save some of the corn meal.

Yellow Perch

The YELLOW PERCH (*Perca flavescens*) like his cousins, the White and Yellow Bass, is strictly a freshwater guy. He is the most widely distributed of all of the Perches, which probably accounts for the fact that he has launched more fishing careers in freshwater than anyone else. From southeastern Canada down through the Carolinas, the Midwest, and many of the states of the Far West, he provides literally hours of fun for vast numbers of fishermen. He definitely prefers cool, clean-water lakes, but once in a while he plays around in large and clean rivers. I would suggest that you look for him any place where there are Small-Mouth Bass, Walleyes, or Pikes. The Yellow Perch is a good fighter and biter and takes a wide variety of lures. Try your small spinners and spoons, but don't go expecting a giant (despite what he might try to make you think with his first tug). Most of these fish go less than a pound, which in a way by relative standards makes a three-pound yellow perch a giant indeed. You might as well treat him as such.

Realize, of course, that this list of freshwater fun fish is necessarily limited. (There are many more species swimming around.) I have simply tried to provide you and your Dad with a guide for "anywhere, anytime" fishing. If you stick to only the fish listed here, I could promise a lifetime of laughs.

A Story About Fun Fish

Writing a story about funfish is almost as hard as writing a story about every breakfast you have—or should have—eaten. There are simply too many. Imagine starting off a story with "Forty years ago on the morning of July 15, I sat down to a breakfast of hot oatmeal and poured orange juice in my bowl by mistake."

On July 16, forty years ago, I sat down to my breakfast and poured orange juice on my oatmeal, because I like it that way. On the morning of the 17 of that month, I sat down to breakfast and poured grape juice on my hot cream of wheat and I hated it."

Well, forty years ago, on July 17th at 2:30 in the afternoon, I caught my first funfish, a fancy and scrappy REDEAR SUNFISH. The following day, I had him for breakfast and never liked cereal with juice, ever again. But pancakes are OK.

The reason I happened to catch a funfish was a book my grandfather had given me, one that he'd had since *he* was young. It was called *The Sportsman's Gazetteer & General Guide*. It was written by Charles Hallock and published in 1883. Mr. Hallock signed his book "Yours Fraternally," which I kind of liked. He also wrote a book a few years earlier (1881), called *Camp Life in Florida*, in which he cautioned sportsmen to keep a sharp eye out for Indians. He signed that one also "Yours Fraternally."

Anyway, my Dad, at my frequent request, would read to me from my "old-timey" book and I loved it—except for one passage, which I set out to disprove. Here is what it said: "From the characteristics and muddy condition of a large proportion of the southern waters, especially in the extreme south, it will be readily perceived why the gentlemen of the south are not anglers."

Well now, I ask you . . .

Later in the book he spoke of my area of Florida, which must have had lovely and friendly Indians, for he never cautioned us once. He said, "One native method of fishing is with a bob, which is a bunch of gay colored feathers, with two or three large hooks concealed in it. This is fastened to a yard or two of strong line, and this to a stout reed pole. The fisherman sits in the bow of a canoe, which is paddled by one on the stern, and kept at such a distance from the weedy shore that the bob may be skittered along the margin. Out rushes the Bass, and cannot well escape being hooked; he is either hauled in by main force, or breaks away."

I decided to give it a try. (I ruined my mother's hat in the process when I collected the gay-colored feathers to make up my bob.) I fished long and hard, skittered like mad; but I guess that because I didn't have a canoe and "one to paddle in the stern," it just wouldn't work. Not a Bass rushed or even looked at my bob, and I never had a chance to use my main force. I suppose now, looking back, that the real trouble might have been my mother's hat which, I suppose, wasn't designed to make bobs.

Anyway, it worked out fine, because I caught my first Stump-knocker breakfast that day on a bent pin and a worm, which I'd taken along just in case and which proved that southern gentlemen *do* like to fish. They just don't like to skitter with bobs.

I fashioned a "bob" out of my mother's hat! It wasn't the smartest "bob" I ever made.

BURR SMIDT

Part Two

•

Saltwater Fishing & Fish

Because the oceans are vast, the life in the sea is varied, and it is no small task that you as a teacher have cut out for yourself.

Just rejoice that your Dad will be quick to catch onto the saltwater fishes. We have narrowed our choices to a mere handful, but what a handful they are! Among them are the strongest, fastest, most beautiful and interesting and, I believe, most sought-after. More important is the fact that, on whichever coast you might find yourself, you also will find at least a few, if not many, of the fishes listed here in your book.

I feel compelled to suggest—though also unhappy to do so—that the best fishing in saltwater is on our East Coast. If you will look at a map for a moment, you'll appreciate why. For one thing, the entire stretch of the Atlantic seaboard is nothing but bays and inlets, rivers and sounds, and literally thousands of islands and harbors, long stretches of marshes and swamps . . . in short: fish habitat. Then too, there's the Gulf Stream, a river of sorts that travels the ocean, swinging in close to the shore with water quite warm enough to affect even the climate. At least, that seems to be the popular belief. I would suggest, however, that the happy effects of warm climate on land are due in large measure to the winds that sweep across the very vast and much warmer waters of the Sargasso Sea, which lies on the ocean flank of the Gulf Stream. At any rate, the Stream is a tropical current that is home or a travel route for millions of fish. Like the Atlantic Coast, the Pacific also has currents that greatly affect either the pleasure or displeasure of fish. The principal current on the West Coast of our country is a southbound extension and branch of the rather chilly Aleutian Current. As it follows south down the American coast, it becomes known as the California Current. And it indeed affects the temperature of the coastal Pacific waters, which tend to be quite cold as compared to the waters back east. Salmon certainly love it, but I doubt if a tropical beach-combing fish would. Actually you might be surprised that the water is cold not for the reason you think, unless you happen to think that it all has something to do with the wind—in which case, you'd be as smart as a Salmon.

What happens is that the prevailing winds off the California coast from March through July cause the *surface* water to flow away from the coast. This, in conjunction with the flow of the California Current, causes an upwelling of the cold bottom waters and subsurface counterflow currents. Actually, despite the fact that it's cool, it does bring up all sorts of important chemicals that react with the sun to provide a rich life-giving environment for fish.

The Pacific Coast, in general, is straight and rocky with but few areas that could be called fish habitat. Of course, as always, there are happy exceptions. For example, within reach of most Californians is the great fishing water of Baja California—down Mexico way—the Sea of Cortez (Gulf of California)—where the fishing rates second to none in the world. And, of course, there is the great and unique sea Salmon fishing up north with its mystery and thrills. But overall for variety and numbers of fish, we have to give the East Coast the edge. And, I might add, Florida has the edge on all that. (Remember that I'm *from* there and naturally partial.)

One of the problems that you as a teacher will run into is the same as the problem that faces me now: Where shall we begin and which shall be the first fish we discuss (I hate playing favorites). I thought perhaps that we might have set up a game of "go fish"—throw all the names in a hat and then just pick out the winner, or then I thought that we might just pick out the guy you are most likely to catch first—but that would depend just where you were and just when, which might not be fair to some other teacher teaching his Dad or someone in some other place.

The Striper

Then who it should be came to me: Mr. Striped Bass, a truly All-American fish. Let me explain some interesting facts about Mr. "Striper." He was on hand when the Pilgrims landed at Plymouth, and he provided a good part of the food that saw them through the lonesome summer of the year 1623. Then in 1670, the Plymouth colonists enacted a law that all revenues derived from the fishing for Striped Bass be used to establish schools for free education in one or another of the towns of the colony. It was the Striped Bass who made it possible to erect the first public school in this, our New World. Many years later, in 1886, he was transplanted to the West, and like the true pioneer that he was he prospered and loved his new home, which was San Francisco and its beautiful bay.

So, my fine teacher of fishing, "rig up your Dad" for a thrill and teach him about this most wonderful of saltwater fishes. You might begin with your usual call: "Hey Dad, I've got a *Roccus saxatilis*" . . . WOW!

And, believe me, if you or your Dad ever get a *Roccus saxatilis* (which is the scientific name for Mr. Striped Bass), you'll really yell "WOW!" that is if, in fact, you have enough strength to do anything. They are strong and can run to a good size, a twenty- or thirty-pounder is not that uncommon. The largest ever recorded was 125 pounds, taken in North Carolina in 1891, but it was not taken on rod and reel and, therefore, is not the record for sportsmen. The sport record stands, where it has been for a good many years, at 73 pounds. This fish was caught in the year 1913 by Mr. C. B. Church in Massachusetts. Both of these large fish were undoubtedly females, which always seem to run larger than males (this is true at any age level). I should think then that any fish over twenty pounds is probably a "cow" and, therefore, at least for myself, I always

I hope you like my picture of this grand guy on page 93.

release the "big" ones. Anyway, fish of ten pounds or less are the best eating. You might suggest to your Dad (after he's caught a few of the biggest and proven the point that he can) that he release all those big cows so that we will always have plenty of these All-American fish.

Remember when I mentioned some fish that live both in the salt and the fresh and all tastes in between? Well, sir, Mr. Striped Bass is just such a fish, normally running up rivers to spawn just like the Salmon, and like the Salmon there are many that live landlocked, in a lake. As a matter of fact, he has been introduced into many lakes in both the East and the West. But don't argue. He is still a saltwater fish and we shall think of and treat him as such.

Tell Dad that the STRIPER is a guy who likes swimming inshore (this is indeed lucky for fishermen). The Striper is rarely caught more than a mile or two off the beach; he prefers hunting his food in the tide rips, rocky shoals, and sand bars, or in sunken islands of grass. His diet is varied, his feeding voracious. He likes all kinds of small fish, such as Herring and Shad, Mullets and Silverside Minnows, Silver Hake and small Flounders and Eels; and like any gourmet who is hungry he eagerly pounces on all types of Lobsters and Crabs and particularly Shrimp and juicy young Clams. His diet certainly sounds like a New England dinner, which leads to a thought that you must tell to Dad, and that is that Old Mr. Striper is a New England fish! Oh, for sure, he wanders down south as far as the north coast of Florida and is even reported around in the Gulf, but for all practical purposes (which is fishing) he is found much further north, from North Carolina to Massachusetts.

One thing to tell Dad that will gladden his heart is that the Striper takes his vacation down on the shore the same time of year that you do. He is a summertime-fall type of fish. It is generally thought that he winters in bays, like the Chesapeake or the Delaware, or in sounds like Albermarle in North Carolina. I also suspect (because I've caught a few winter fish in the North) that some hang around in deeper water off shore through the winter, just out of reach. Come early spring, the Striper starts his vacation or migration (whichever you choose) and begins moving north looking for proper rivers and places to spawn. It follows with logic then that the greatest concentrations of fish occur progressively later (by month) as we move up the coast into the North. Tell Dad that, come June, he'll catch fish only at the southern end of the range, but come August, September, that's the best time for the New England Coast and the time to take all of those big ones. The Pacific Stripers do not have the great migrations that are known in the East. They generally move into the Sacramento-San Joaquin River delta to spend their winters in freshwater. They then move out in the spring to spawn in the delta, spending their summers in the San Francisco Bay area, where they are caught in both salt and brackish waters.

Almost all of my Striper fishing experiences have been in the East, so naturally I shall concentrate most of the lesson for you to teach Dad on the waters I know and the lures that for me have proven best. I've been assured that the Striper, when he made his move as a pioneer out to the West, took all his preferences and habits along. Therefore, most undoubtedly would be fished quite the same.

As you might have guessed by now, reading the menu preferred by a fish gives you a clue to the type or types of lure they'd prefer. In the case of the Striper, you have wide latitude. You can almost never go wrong if you stick to lures that represent small fish (this, of course, in the case of the Striper includes lures that look and act like the eel). Stripers will hit surface, shallow, and deep-running lures. My personal thought is that most of the big fish are taken down near the bottom. For that reason I use my all-around favorite saltwater lure, a bucktail jig. It can be fished a number of ways to simulate a number of types of gourmet dishes that appeal to the Striper. It can be worked to act like a Shrimp or a Squid or a fast-swimming Minnow or one that has been crippled and seems to a Bass quite easy to take. Stripers are taken right off of the beach. When you fish for them this way you are surf casting, and it's a wonderful way to take this great fish. It's a lonely, waiting game (be prepared), as Stripers travel in schools. As a rule you must wait for the fish to show, or get in a beach buggy and go out and find them where they are feeding—just behind the breakers offshore near the bars—and you will have some fine feathered friends that will help you. Just look for the birds as they circle and scream (they get as excited as you). When you see those gulls and terns wheeling and diving, swooping low, you can be sure that there are Stripers or Bluefish feeding below. Have your Dad get his lure out and quickly give it the action. He'll be into a fine fighting fish before he can guess just what is going to happen. You notice that I've mentioned "or Bluefish." Explain to Dad that Bluefish and Stripers travel similar routes and seasons. (You'll learn all about Bluefish in the very next chapter.)

One of my favorite ways to fish Stripers is from a small boat. I'm sure that you and your Dad will like fishing this way too. Early in the morning, when I 'm in time to enjoy the sunrise and its color (my favorite time), I like to go out in the Bay or the Sound and poke around rocks and little grassy islands where there are dropoffs into deeper water (it needn't be too deep). It helps if the water is clean, as both you and the fish will like it better that way. It also helps if you can find a spot where the tide runs a bit stronger. Stripers prefer strong running water, and they even like water that's too rough for me to enjoy (it naturally depends on the spot that you find). Cast out slightly uptide with a bucktail and bring your lure back rather slowly close to the bottom; then give a lift to your rod (double twitch) and then bow, letting the lure settle down toward the bottom. Then repeat double twitch: this gives your bucktail the action. Sometimes it helps to use a pork rind attached to your hook.

You can buy these by the jar in any tackle store in the East; some of the prepared rinds have a tail hook already attached. Use them; they are good for fish that hit short, missing the hook. If there are Stripers known to be around the area where you fish, this technique will almost always take them. If it seems slow (and Striper fishing can be), try a bit of trolling, moving quite slowly (when you think that you are moving too slow, it's just about right). Most of the action is imparted by you to the lure; just keep up a twitch and a jerk. Stripers always seem (at least to me) to hit when you least expect them. You might get discouraged and then whammo! You're on.

These are very strong fish. Don't try to "horse" them; your drag should be reasonably light, as a big fish can easily snap a line that tests out heavier than the fish weighs. For example, a thirty-pound Striper can part a line of forty-five pounds of test before you have time to know what you've hooked. Conversely, of course, you can handle a large fish on eight-pound test line; just let the drag and the rod do most of the work. I seldom go heavier than ten pounds of test when spinning for Stripers; however, do go for a heavier leader, about twenty to twenty-five pounds of monofilament line three feet long. Without it, a large Striper can part your light line with a flick of his tail as he runs, or quite often when hooked he will roll at the surface near the end of a fight. Stripers are very active at night and many "Striper specialists" fish them only at that time, preferably when the tide is at flood. I must admit that I've fished often at night and caught Stripers, but I also admit that it scares me a bit, hooking something as big as a "cow" Striper and not being able to follow the action. You feel very awed and certainly helpless. If you enjoy thrills, feeling a tiny bit scared, take Dad fishing for Stripers at night. Night fishing can also be great from the beach, but then I like to use lures that pop on the surface; you can follow the action. A couple of good lures for this type of top-water fishing are the Point Jude pop-along or the Atom or Phillips 77. Don't forget to try the old standby Rapala in the Saltwater Magnum sizes. They are hard to beat.

If Dad fell in love when you taught him to *fly* fish for Trout and you have a hard time getting him to put his flyrod away when you head for the coast and vacation, don't worry at all. Just see that he has a larger flyrod and send him off fishing for Stripers. Stripers are one of a handful of saltwater fish that are ideal to take on a flyrod. Tell your Dad to use either popping bugs or streamers. I personally prefer the streamers, generally those tied with a good deal of white. Some typical patterns would be the Bonbright Streamer, the Gibbs Striper Bucktail, the Pflueger Shark Fly. Sometimes yellow is the best of all colors—Phillips puts one out called the Bead Head—it is yellow and red and works wonders. Tell Dad that the conditions for *fly* casting would be about the same as when he went out early morning in a small boat and was fishing with spinning gear and

Check them out on the following page.

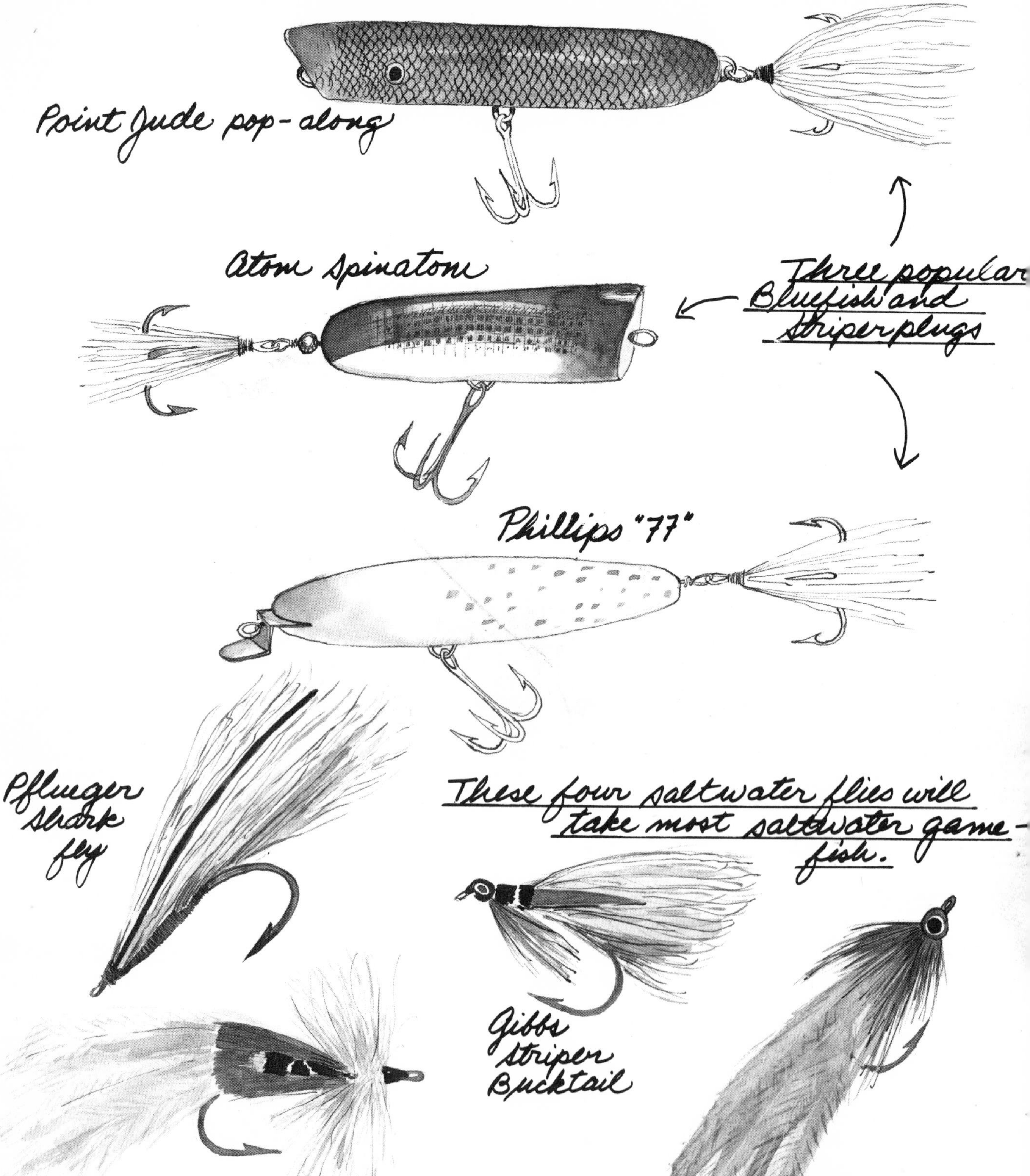

Point Jude pop-along

Atom spinatone

Three popular Bluefish and striper plugs

Phillips "77"

Pflueger shark fly

These four saltwater flies will take most saltwater game-fish.

Gibbs Striper Bucktail

Bonbright streamer

Phillips Bead head

bucktail jig along the tide rips and shallow water near dropoffs and those grassy islands we mentioned. Retrieve his fly with one- or two-foot jerks; keep it moving and quite animated. When using poppers let him use the same general technique that he would use on freshwater Black Bass. Give it a twitch and then rest; a jiggle, a twitch, and a rest. When a Striper hits, he hits with a vengeance, so tell your Dad to calm down and hold on. Another hint that you might pass on to Dad is that whenever you drive on the East Coast and find yourself crossing even small bridges out to the islands across cuts that move pretty well with the tide and have marshes around, these are prime areas for fishing for Stripers, particularly in late summer and into the fall. If you are particularly lucky and hear an old timer speak of some "hot spot" for Stripers, give it a try. Stripers seem to frequent the same spots year after year. I would venture to say that even some spots that were good for the Pilgrims are good to this day. Caution: don't count on finding one of *these* Old Timers, the Pilgrims, (you won't), just settle for someone who really loves fishing for Stripers; they always seem ready to help. Hooray for old fishermen and Stripers.

A Story About Striped Bass

The first time I caught a Striped Bass had nothing to do with what I thought I was doing. I had no help from an Old Timer or anyone else, except maybe a book.

I had gone fishing for Weakfish (which are not weak at all except in the mouth). I had moved from my Florida home to the Connecticut shore, the beautiful town of Westport on Long Island Sound.

I knew nothing of New England fish—what a strange clan they were to a Florida boy—Tautog and Cod, bait-stealing Cunners and Skates. One fish, however, stood out in my mind and that was the Weakfish, for he was a cousin to a fish that I love and had taught my Dad how to catch in the South, Mr. Spotted Seatrout. The book that I'd read had suggested that both of these fish liked the same type of lures and similar waters (though I don't know quite for sure). At a glance I could find little in common with Long Island Sound and the Gulf, except that they were wet. I chose for my lure a bucktail type jig, for it had always proved deadly down home on the "trout," and I believed in the book (with reservations, of course, about its comments about water.)

There was another fish in the book that appealed to me greatly. This was the Striper. Not only was he a beautiful fish, but he looked as strong as a fish could be strong. A "specialist's" fish, said the book and centered its theme on fishing for this fish in the surf at Cape Cod. The Striper became just a dream for the future. I wasn't a "specialist" and I was a long way from Cape Cod. I put all the dreams to one side and went fishing for Weaks off of Westport. In a small rented skiff with an outboard, I made my way out to one of the small islands that lay less than a mile off the shore. I decided to troll, the better to learn the lay of the land, or the water as it was in this case. The "lay" came as quite a surprise; it was water somewhat similar to what I had known. It was certainly colder, for sure, but it was clean and quite clear and on the windward side of the small rock island there were reefs—not quite like the reefs that I knew from the past—but undoubtedly reefs, large rocks that pushed up to the surface, providing a fish haven for fish. On the lee side of the island the water was shallow (2 to 4 feet) and I could see that there were patches of grass like that in the bay down home that the Seatrout loved with a passion. So, I trolled, and my excitement began to mount. Conditions were perfect. I'd catch Weakfish for sure. Every second I expected a strike, every second for the next two hours. Once I caught the edge of the reef and my excitement knew no bounds at the action.

I guess finally I was ready to give it all up, call it a day. I felt terribly sorry for these poor New Englanders: pretty water, no fish.

That's about the thought that I held when it happened: I was literally jolted from my arms to my toes—my reel screamed in torment—as the fish whatever he was (and I knew that it wasn't a "Weakfish" . . . they didn't grow to such weight) took off at a good steady clip paralleling the island and heading up north for Cape Cod. I held the rod with one hand as it bent double. I knew that I had to follow the fish with the boat, as my line was running off my reel uncomfortably steadily and fast. With my free hand I managed to get the boat turned and headed at a good clip after the fish, not too good a clip, however, but just enough to keep the pressure on. Ten minutes later the fish broached, came to the surface and rolled. I couldn't make out what he was, but the swirl he left on the surface was scary, like a whirlpool of awesome dimension. I would guess that I fought that fish for another ten minutes or so with the boat

I knew it wasn't a Weakfish!

BURR SMIDT

before I knew I was winning; or rather, I began to have hopes that I'd win, for although he still had power control of the play, I was gaining back line.

It's a truth that when you deal with a fish of this size you can never be sure that you've won until he's safe on the deck of the boat. Although I am full as any fisherman with tales of fish that jump over the moon and run away with the spoon or what ever else they may have decided to take, in this case I felt that he *could* jump over the moon.

I had caught my first Striper in a shower of spray at the side of the boat. I had reached down and slid two fingers in his gills and my thumb in his mouth, and I lifted his thirty-three pounds high in the air with a shout.

In many ways I supposed, I was proudest of this fish of all that I've caught. At least I was if one can measure the weight of memories. Every detail of the day stands vivid in mind and it's been twenty-eight years; I even remember a little nick in the head of the bucktail I used. I certainly remember the look of the guy at the dock when I returned. He was stunned.

I remember my Dad's smile and his first words after he saw the great fish I'd caught. "I see you've gone out and caught one of your dreams."

"Yes, sir," I said. "Next time we'll have the pleasure together!" And we did.

Striped Bass

Chasing a "Bucktail"

BURR SMOT

Bucktail
with a "tail hook"
pork rind
attacher.

The Little Pickerels:
These little fellows are of
no interest to fishermen!
If you catch one, always
let him go. It might
just be a baby muskellunge,
and you certainly want
him to grow
up!

93

The Bluefish

He is feeding on one of his
favorite dinners, the Atlantic
menhaden or "Bunker".

There were a couple of bait fishermen working on the bridge when I arrived. I had seen neither before, which made them fair sport.

"How they biting?" I asked as I leaned my bike on the rail.

"Got a couple," the nearest man answered, "but they sure aren't doing too good; too much bait in the water, I guess." He smiled sadly.

"Reckon you're right about that," said I, knowing full well that this *was* the case, that fish often refused a baited hook when there was an abundance of natural free-swimmers about. I geared up for my next innocent shaft. I held up my dude, a beat-up old lure in white that had taken more than its fair share of Mackerel. "How's something like this for them fish?" I asked, looking bewildered and even younger than ten, yet knowing that in a very short time I'd be walking away with at least twenty-some cents worth of fish.

"Well, son," he replied very friendly, "I wouldn't think so . . . you'd do better with some natural fresh bait."

"I haven't any," I said.

"Here, help yourself," he replied, indicating his bucket of lifeless Sardines.

"I was beginning to feel guilty about putting him on. "Reckon not. I think I'll just give this here thing a try." I paused and then quickly added my thanks. He dribbled in some Chum and went back to his fishing. I backed off a bit and gave a really good cast. My lure landed near where his Chum line thinned out. I started to whip, sure that I'd take a fish on my very first cast, which I didn't. Nor did I get so much as a strike for the next hour, a failing which left me with terribly mixed emotions. On the one hand I was glad that I hadn't shown up my new friend; but deep in my fisherman's heart I was a little destroyed because I had not. I don't suppose that it helped a whole lot when my baitfishing friend and his partner each took a couple more fish.

The worst of it all was that the hour for school was creeping up fast and I'd have to go. I threw out my very last cast. As I whipped the line in, I turned to my friend to wish him good luck . . . and the mighty fish hit. So you can see that all my intentions were good; I had no choice but to cut class what with the crowd and the yelling and the fact that the fish was too big for my bike. My Father forgave me right off the top when he saw my big Mackerel; for that I was exceedingly grateful. The only bad thing I can remember is that I missed my second sailing with Columbus and a sea filled to overflowing with Mackerel.

The Snook

Now get that name right, it is Snook and not *Schnook.*

A SNOOK is a wonderful fish; a schnook is a klutz who's never learned about fishing, but could; and if he did would be an ex-schnook, which is okay (we were, at one time, all of us, schnooks).

Let's put a couple of tricks in Dad's fishing bag and teach him all about Snook. (Rest assured that he'll need all of your tricks and a few more.)

Have your Dad yell out (this is a practice): "Hey, Little Pal! I've got a *Centropomus undecimalis* on." With a scientific name like that he'll need all the practice he can get. In reality, when practice is over and you have managed to get your Dad tied on to one of these fish, his yell will probably be more graphic and down to earth, like the following example: "Hey . . . Hey . . . Hey, Help! Hey Little Pal . . . I gotmeasnook!"

The Snook is a warm-water fish, and the warmest water we have is off Florida; that's where you'll go to fish Mr. Snook.

Explain to your Dad that there are a number of species of Snook, but because some are so rare or of such small size they are of little importance to us. The one that we shall discuss is the one listed above. We shall call him the FLORIDA SNOOK, but let's for the fun and the knowledge meet some of his family. They all can be caught and you just might.

mr. Snook's picture is on page 128.

One of the Snooks that grows to a fairly good size is the BLACK SNOOK, who lives in the West. He is found south of our borders from the Sea of Cortez down to Ecuador. He seems to be fairly common through much of his range, although he is nowhere near as common as the Florida Snook is in his.

There are three other Snooks that we know something about. They are found in Florida, but all three are quite small and relatively rare, at least in that state. They seem to prefer a more southerly range and even warmer water than the Florida Snook, more down the West Indies way.

They are:

The LITTLE SNOOK, who, despite his name, is second in size on the East Coast to the mighty Florida guy. But, I have to report that he runs a mighty poor second at that; he seldom reaches a weight of over five or six pounds, while the Florida Snook can and does go over fifty.

The TARPON SNOOK is smaller yet. A couple of pounds is for him a very good size, but he takes a fly or lure well, and is fun on ultra-light tackle.

The SWORDSPINE SNOOK is the smallest and rarest of all. If you were to take a wee, tiny feller less than a foot, I'd suspect that you'd lucked into this guy.

Let's put the midgets aside and talk about the Florida Snook, which is the one that you want and the one that you'll most likely catch. (Everyone wants to catch the Florida Snook. He's a very glamorous guy. Even schnooks want to catch Snook, when they hear some of the stories about him.)

As I hinted before, the Snook grows to a pretty good size. A number of fish have been taken that exceed the fifty-pound mark. His average however will be somewhere between ten and twenty pounds. Thirty-pounders are not all that uncommon.

The Snook is an inshore-type swimmer and seldom ventures far from the beach. He loves bays and canals and is fond of playing up those Florida rivers that turn into freshwater. As a matter of fact, you will find a few truly big fish right in the fresh at the source of the rivers. He likes pilings and posts and oyster beds; he hangs around reefs and seems to like bridges (not to cross over but to play under). He seems particularly fond of the little "humpyback" bridges that cross the canals and lagoons. In the summer at evening you'll spot him swimming along off the beaches with a couple of pals; this is particularly true of the beach passes. He'll be out just a couple of feet from the shore in water that seems almost too shallow for swimming. Or if you know of a spot that has mangroves that grow down to the edge near fairly deep water, you have found one of his haunts, where he hunts for his food. (If you don't know about the mangrove, look for a bush with shiny, waxy leaves that grows with a tangle of roots right into the water.) Around mangroves, a Snook is usually assured of finding a meal of Mullet or Grunts or Snappers and Crabs. They are all part of his diet, though he seems to prefer schooling-type Minnows like the Sardines. (I would guess that they are an easier harvest.)

Now that we know that the Snook doesn't eat grapefruit, I guess it's time for you to talk to your Dad about lures.

As we've mentioned before when we've talked about fish that have a diet like his (the Bluefish, for an example), what you need for

Snook are Minnow or small fishy-type lures, the plugs and the bucktails and nylon "dude" jigs. Snook will also take spoons and flashy-type metal. (In my opinion the metal type lures are not quite as good.)

Think of the tricks you learned when you fished for Black Bass in freshwater, add a few tricks you picked up fishing for Mackerel, and you should be able to go out and catch Snook. Use spinning or baitcasting tackle; it should be just a bit heavier than what you were using on Bass. The tip of your rod should have a little more stiffness than usual. Two points support this suggestion: one is that the Snook has a pretty tough mouth and you have to really get a bit tough yourself when you are setting the hook. The second reason for a rod with stiffer action is the manner of working the lure. This is particularly true of topwater plugs; you must use a somewhat modified form of the whip that you learned fishing for Mackerel. The stiffness is needed because of the weight of the lure you'll be fishing, considerably heavier than the ones that you used on the Mackerel.

You want a vigorous action, but not quite as fast as the action you used to take Mackerel. You want your plug to jump and dart from side to side; keep it moving, and keep up the pretense that it's a small fish running in panic. Use the same forceful style when fishing your bucktails and dudes. Deep-running plugs usually have an action built in, but sometimes for Snook it's not quite enough. Add a little dance of your own. Believe me, it won't hurt a thing. The color that Snook seem to prefer in your bucktails and dudes are red and white or all white when you are fishing the clean open-type water like that found in the passes or the Gulf. When you move into the bays and the bayous and up around the mangroves and oyster beds where the water tends to run slightly to yellow or even a light coffee brown, then you should change your lures to yellow and white or all yellow and be right in style.

Without question the best time to fish Snook is in the evening and on into the night. But don't give up your early mornings; they are good too. As a matter of fact, play it safe and fish both ends of the day. What the tide is up to is often a clue as to the best place to look for the Snook. In a way, like a lot about fishing, it's just common sense: figuring out the conditions that will provide these smart fish with a meal. For example, if you are going to be up a creek, the best time to be there would be on an incoming tide (everything comes in with the tide); if the tide is on its way out and the water falls rather fast, that's the time to be down at the *mouth* of the creek, near a deep hole where a Snook will be waiting for the tide to bring out a dinner (everything goes out with the tide). Although it's of lesser importance, when fishing the ocean or Gulf, I prefer the tide at the flood or just moving out. The bottom near shore seems to be a little more fertile at this point, and the bait hangs around trying to keep near the shore. The bonus, of course, is that as the tide runs out you can keep working closer to good spots that you know that are there and couldn't quite reach a couple of hours ago.

Snook seem to spawn through most of the summer, but on a few of the trips that I took when I was a kid, I noticed, back up in the deep piney woods and palmettos, quite a way in from the shore, places where I found small tributaries or creeks that looked more like ditches, in which milling about were any number of really big Snook. I suspect they were up there on mass spawning runs. It was always in the fall, about September, just before school. I would suggest that, if you run into something like that, don't try to catch them. Just sit down with Dad, watch, and enjoy—maybe applaud.

Naturally, when you start talking about things you remember from a long time ago, it's hard to stop. It's like opening up a whole can of lures.

One thing I remember that you and your Dad will enjoy is a way we used to catch Snook. It's certainly not as sporting as a light rod and reel, but it's fun and you can learn quite a lot about more than just Snook. It's a technique called "figure-eighting." It may well be a lost art, even in Florida, but I'm sure that there are a lot of old timers about who will give a big smile when they remember.

You should fish off a bridge at night, one that's not very high. It should span a body of water that you know holds some Snook. Get a Calcutta cane pole about twelve feet in length (it should be a really good strong one), tie on a piece of strong leader wire about one foot in length, and to that add your lure, a good top water plug. (When I was a kid, we used to use about four or five inches off the end of a broom handle, to which we had screwed on a good sturdy hook.) Now get a good Coleman gas lantern and tie on a long cord. Lower it over the side until it hangs two feet or so off of the water. It should cast a good circle of light, about four feet in diameter. Okay. Now lean over the side of the bridge, and don't fall off. Tilt your pole straight down until your plug rests on the water. Start to weave a good figure-eight with your plug. The length of the figure can be anything up to about four feet. Keep it going fairly fast, at least fast enough to create a reasonable commotion as it moves. Keep your action close to your lantern, just a few feet away. The lantern is there to attract all sorts of goodies. They'll come in like moths to a flame. In will come Shrimp and some Squid and Minnows, of course, and there on the outside of the circle of light you will start to see some fairly large shadows assemble.

Every now and then, one of the shadows will come tearing in after some food. It might be a Ladyfish or a Tarpon or the largest Spotted Trout you've ever seen. Any one of them might hit your plug, but the chances are good that after a while a big Snook will come charging out from under the bridge. He will try to pull your Dad into the water, but he won't if you have taken the time to tell Dad to be careful. (Most dads are anyway, so don't worry.)

Here is a list of lures and a caution to give Dad.

The *caution* first: Use a leader. It needn't be long, about 6 to 8 inches of *wire* will do. "Hey," you might say, "a Snook ain't got no teeth!" Well, you are correct about that; it's just that your language is wrong. "A Snook has no teeth" is a better way to put it. The wire is there because a Snook carries a *razor.* At least he carries a flat bony plate that's as sharp as a razor. It is there on his gill plate, and you'd better watch out. Be careful of your fingers.

About plugs: Every Snook fisherman soon develops a favorite. Usually the favorite is the last one he took a fish on, which only goes to show that a Snook doesn't turn up his nose at too many plugs. I suppose they have favorites also, but generally speaking any well-made saltwater-type plug that will chug and or pop or can be made to do so will take Snook. The action that you will give it is more important.

There is one plug that's been a standby for Snook fishermen for many a year. I hope you can find one. It's called "Calico Bill." It's orangy yellow, with touches of black and some stripes and some dots, and it sounds perfectly gruesome. It is not. I wouldn't go fishing without at least one silver or gold Rapala, in a 13 Magnum floating model, and don't forget to carry bucktails and some dudes in the colors already suggested. These latter should be about one ounce or slightly less. Despite the fact that a Snook has a huge appetite and a mouth to match, like most big fish, sometimes he seems to prefer smaller lures or perhaps is less scared when you cast.

A Story About Snook

It would be a mistake to say to a Snook, "Don't go getting so personal." They are a very personal fish and will butt their noses into your business whenever it pleases their fancy. They are by nature quite rude and, as a result, will often act boorish and nasty. What I don't understand is why I so love them when they are acting that way, and wouldn't give two hoots a fin and a tail for gnarly old or young people who do quite the same.

The first Snook I met was a crusty buttinski indeed. I was nine and, as is the trait of that age, I was definitely minding my own business, down on the end of the dock my Dad had built out in front of our house. My business was catching Sardines. Looking back with an unbiased perspective that has developed over the years, I can truthfully say I knew my business quite well and it was thriving. I'd also admit, if you were to ask me today, that my methods of business were somewhat substandard from the standpoint of sport. I was snitching Sardines with a small treble hook tied by black carpet-thread to the end of a fragile and green fresh-cut stick of bamboo, so fragile it would bend nearly double from the weight of two ounces of foul-hooked Sardine.

The water was crystalline, clear like a spring, a condition that prevailed only once in a while during the summer. I could see straight to the bottom, which I imagined was of far greater depth than it was. Thoughts of a bottomless sea flashed through my mind. (A strange paradox of great moment, for such thoughts struck me only at times when, in fact, I could see to the bottom.)

The Sardine business was spotty at best on this day. They were about in great numbers, as was usual, but for some reason they were traveling about in small, fragmented schools. I would coax in the schools as they passed the dock with a handful of bread crumbs, and as they bunched up to feed I'd start in on my snitching. The technique was effective. I'd lower my deadly three-pointed hook to a depth just below where they fed. They would bump and nip at the line, for whatever reason a Sardine might have, which is reason enough I suppose. I'd bring the hook up with a jerk and hope for the best, which "best" was, of course, to impale a smaller silver fish on my hook for my own reasons. This seemed only fair, since I've already ceded the right of Sardines to behave as they did as "reason enough"; ditto for me. I think you might have gathered, by now, my philosophy regarding "buttinskis." I didn't get rude and ask the Sardines WHY they butted and nipped at the line. I just snitched and, of course, I wouldn't have welcomed anyone boorish enough to ask, "Why are you snitching sardines?" Like I said, "I did it for reason enough!"

But since I am sure that you are not rude and wouldn't dare ask such a personal question, I'll tell you: I snitched them for bait.

On one of my snitches I missed a Sardine but got a hook full of his tiny scales; they floated through the water looking like flecks of pure silver. It was then that I caught sight of the Snook and for one fleeting moment was scared. I guess it would be better to say I experienced shock or excitement, perhaps even a bit of all three: scare, shock, excitement. Then a funny thing happened that I still can't explain. I knew with a certainty that he'd been there awhile just staring at me, and now that I'd seen him we both continued to stare; I knew that we had instant rapport. It seems silly to say I knew what he thought, for thought suggests reason; but I knew what he thought. He was deeply aware of me . . . every detail . . . and showed absolutely no fear.

I'm sure that he studied my small fishing rig and laughed to himself. He seemed to study my small skinny boy arms and to laugh even more. I knew he was thinking about when to butt in and just how rude he would be. He moved very slowly off to his left, but he kept his eyes deadlocked with mine; I could see a small school of Sardines heading our way. I moved as slowly and as smoothly as the Snook had. Although my heart was like a triphammer beating away and pumping up blood that was too thick to pass through my veins, I was almost sick with excitement—and still he just stared. I knew he was just waiting for me to do all the work, to catch a Sardine. I dribbled in bread crumbs and quietly lowered my line into position. I felt the Sardines start to rap at the line. I was ready.

I could see the Snook edging in closer. It seemed that we were a team and I could sense him trying to tell me when I should snitch . . . NOW! . . . jerk . . . was his message. (I wished he had put it some other way like, "Now . . . JERK!") I came up on the pole and hooked a Sardine, which for a very short moment fluttered about. I shut my eyes because I knew he was coming, taking control, butting in. He came straight out of the water, shaking his head, my hook deep in the side of his jaw, where he and I both knew it would be. I leaned out over the edge of the dock, held out my arms and my pole to give slack and he came back down to the water. I guess my maneuver surprised him a bit. He had planned to break my line when he hit; he even started to swim off slowly. So sure was he that he had completed the act that when he realized that I had indeed won the first round he tore into a rage.

Then he made another mistake. He came charging toward me, by the side of the dock, straight for the beach. But I was too smart and I

A Story About Bonefish

It wouldn't be right to fault people who came through the Great Depression for having funny ideas about fish, like, for example, most of the folks from the town where I lived as a boy. They thought that a fish that wasn't good on the table certainly wasn't any good for anything else. It didn't matter a bit whether or not that fish might have been smart or could fight like a riled-up old tiger. I suppose that if you were to apply that same notion to folks, very few would have survived the Depression. One of the victims of such tom-foolish thought was the Bonefish, and looking back I guess I would have to include myself, if for no other reason than that, because he was no good to eat, I didn't meet him until there were hamburgers and chicken around once again. I was twelve.

I first knew the Bonefish by another name, one that was Spanish. We called him Macabí, a pretty good romantic and fishy-type name. I have no doubt at all that, if he were called that today, there would be gourmets standing in line for "Fresh Filet Almandine Macabí" or "Macabí Head and Bone Chowder." How delicious it sounds! Being perfectly honest and putting menus and depressions aside, and notwithstanding what folks might have thought, the simple fact is that had I the chance I'd have caught all the Bonefish that swam. Bonefish but rarely (which almost means "never") swam as far north as my home and I even more rarely swam, walked, or drove down to theirs in the Keys. Macabí chowder or not, I never had much of a chance until I was twelve and my Dad drove us down to the Keys.

Just in case you might not have noticed or even given thought to the fact that certain ideas die rather hard (tom-foolish or not), consider this now: we did not, I repeat, *did not,* go down to the Keys to fish Macabí or anything else that wasn't good on the table. We drove down strictly on business; my Dad had set up a deal for marketing Lobsters (the spiny Florida kind without claws) and, as Key West was the center of this delicious and crustaceous trade, we went there. My Dad needed to work out the supply and shipment of this seafood staple. He took me along for my humble support and advice, and I might add, with all due humility, that it was lucky for him that he did. It was I who brought along a couple of baitcasting rods just in case we might find the time to catch Snappers, which by anyone's standards were the best eating of all.

We drove down through the Everglades, which is Seminole Indian land and a wonderful and mysterious swamp filled with great cypress trees and millions of beautiful birds. Our car was a 1938 Ford and practically new, which, of course, means it still had the "smell." The newish Ford was at least half the adventure.

We crossed to the Keys at Key Largo and started on down the string of small islands, the fishiest drive in all of this world: nothing but beautiful water and bridges that span tropical islets of coral and sand. You could look out over the water and just *feel* all the fish, a fact that was driving me crazy, because my Dad wouldn't stop. Oh, I knew that business is business; I knew about meetings and all of that stuff; but still I would die every time we crossed over a bridge or drove close to the water. I would sigh, saying with dull repetition, "Looks kinda good over there!" Sometimes I'd point and then settle back, totally destroyed, as we moved right along: *"Looked* kinda good!" I'd observe, juggling my commentator's style midway between "accuse" and "despair."

When Dad had completed his business and assured a supply of sweet-tasting Lobsters for the folks back up home who were tired of Mullet and grits, we went fishing. One of the fishermen, Capt. Pindar, we had been dealing with took us to his small fishing camp on one of the Keys a few miles to the north. It was called No Name Key, which I considered a pretty good name.

We arrived at No Name in late afternoon, as so often happens when you are all fired up and particularly anxious to get started on fun. I had to wait.

"Wait until morning," they said.

"It's getting too late," they said.

"We'll go out for Snappers come morning. We'll have an early breakfast and get a good start," they said.

Of course as you might suspect, I thought differently. After having waited so long, and with all that water that looked so wonderfully fishy right at my feet, I spoke up (with respect): "I'd like to go fishing *RIGHT NOW!*"

Everything came to a stop for a moment; I think that they were impressed by my frankness and tone of respect. (As it turned out, whether they were or were not, at least they understood with a smile.)

Our fisherman friend told me that the really good Snapper fishing was a couple of miles away and that we'd go out in the morning by boat, but that if I didn't care about good eating fish and didn't mind wading, right there in front of the camp out on the flats I could have all sorts of afternoon fun. "You'll pick up plenty of Jacks and there are Macabí, if you're good."

Down at the end of his dock he had a big bait box made out of wire and wood, more than half full with large and lively Florida Shrimp. I took out a dozen and put them in a floating bait pail, which I tied with some string to my belt. I took out one of our bait-casting rods, tied on a very fine leader and hook. I said good-bye; they wished me good luck; and I started to wade out from the camp. I don't suppose I'd made ten or twelve yards when a big Barracuda came out of nowhere and decided to tag along off to one side.

Well, I suppose I am brave, but certainly not uncommonly so. I was, to mention it mildly, commonly scared. I looked around for support, some kind of weapon lying about on the bottom, an old

I prepared to defend myself!

BONEFISH • 133

conch shell, anything would have done. I pointed my rod tip down and into the water, aiming at the big fish. I was prepared to defend myself. Then I called, with all the calm I could muster, to my Dad and Capt. Pindar, who were watching me from the shore. I wanted to yell "HELP!" but I didn't. My voice simply cracked when I said—as I wished to myself that I'd waited for morning—"Dad! There's a big Barracuda out here!"

I waited, holding my breath, for the report to sink in. "Don't scare him too much," said my Dad. The thought crossed my mind that perhaps I'd made too much of a pest of myself about fishing as we had come down through the Keys.

"Hey! HEY! Dad, what should I do?"

"He's not out to bother you, son. He's just a mite curious. Pay him no mind; he'll soon go away."

"He's mighty big," I quavered.

"Your Dad is telling you true," said Capt. Pindar. Then he added, "You just wade on over toward him and watch him scoot out of your way."

Well, there didn't seem to be more help than that coming, so I gave it a shot. I waded right toward that fish and, sure enough, when I closed to about ten feet away, he sidled around in a sneaky fish turn and glided away. My Dad called out some advice when he saw my relief: "You're liable to meet quite a few of those fellows out there. If it bothers you, son, come on in. Most anyone would. But believe me, they are just very curious. The most trouble he's likely to give is to steal a hooked fish."

Now, since I had survived with only small damage to the pit of my stomach, I decided to go on and fish. Quite naturally my eyes became uncommonly sharp that afternoon and they darted about almost beyond my control, which was good, for soon they spotted, fifteen yards off to my right, eight or nine shadows cruising along. At first I thought perhaps they were Mullet, but their movements were far less erratic and nobody jumped (which Mullet constantly do as they look for danger below). I knew they definitely were some fish other than Mullet, so I hooked up a Shrimp and cast out and ahead of the school. All I can say is that I wasn't prepared for what happened. When the fish took the bait and made his first run, it was beyond the edge of my dreams about great fighting fish, beyond my experience with Tarpon and Snook. I forgot about the morning to come and the Snappers. I forgot about the days of frustration just passed. I had never hooked such a fish, never dreamed that fish could make such a speed; my line cut the water and whistled. I stood there with my rod held up high and tried to brake the outgoing line with my thumb to the spool

I fought him for near twenty minutes and finally won. I was surprised by his size, which certainly wasn't impressive: maybe six, perhaps seven, pounds of pure silver. My first Macabí! Of course I didn't know who he was at the time and didn't until I had brought him ashore. My Dad explained about Bonefish and food. Like the Jack and some of the fun fish, when you catch one, "the White Fox of the Marl," let him go.

Later my Dad wondered aloud why not even once had I mentioned my run-in with the Great Barracuda, and I said, and quite honestly so, "I'd forgot."

Tarpon

"Once upon a time ". . . That is the way we should begin the lesson for Dad about this most amazing of fish. Of course, we must realize that if we do we are committed to the "mandate," that a story must follow. Usually these are stories about princes and frogs—like the time a prince stepped on a frog's toe and was turned into a wart . . . or something like that. (Everybody but frogs know that these stories are pure poppycock.)

With a story about Tarpon, you'd have to come up with something that everyone would believe. For example: Zeus (as he was called by the Greeks) was a fish of great powers that belonged to the family of fish called Zeidae. All of the fish of the sea would come to the foot of his oyster-shell throne and beg for all sorts of special considerations; some wanted to be strong, others petitioned to be at least as fast as a rocket, some asked to have swords, and so on. One fish, a small Herring-type fellow, didn't give two scales and a fin about Zeus and Zeus knew it, which made him terribly mad. He decided to get rid of the Tarpon (that was this one fish's name). He thought and he thought and finally decided to make him a BIG fish in a very small pond on the backside of Mars. He blew Tarpon up to a very respectable size (200-plus pounds) and had him silver-plated (for safe entry into Mars' atmosphere). He gave the Tarpon a mighty toss by the tail, straight for the planet. But as factual stories will have it, his plan went awry and the Tarpon fell short of the target, landing in a mysterious body of water unknown to Zeus, which turned out to be off the Gulf Coast of Florida. The Tarpon was made and remains so to this day. (Secretly he had wanted to be a big fish in a small pond, but not up on Mars.) As in all "Once upon a time" stories, happy endings prevail. In time he grew to love his new home; he was proud of his size and doubly so when it came to his bright silver-plating. That is why, to this day, when you hook him he fights like ten tigers to stay where he is. Perhaps he's convinced that you've been sent there by Zeus to send him to Mars (which today is a practical trip, so who can blame him for what he believes?).

Of course, the only truth in this whole fishy tale is everything—except about Mars, where there are no small ponds that we now of. This is the time to get your Dad's fullest attention (when he starts fishing for Tarpon, you may never get it again). Ask Dad, "Who's Zeus?" Be prepared for the answer he'll give, "Zeus who?" because afterward you are going to shock him with knowledge and sageness guaranteed to give you the stage. He will say something like: "Zeus was the supreme deity of the ancient Greeks, husband of Hera . . ." Smile and nod your head yes, and then say, "Sure dad, everyone knows about those old *myths*" (be sure you stress *myths*) after which you continue, "The Zeus in that story is quite *real*" (stress *real,* and explain) "he's not related anyway at all to the Tarpon. His common name as a matter of fact is the John Dory *(Zeus faber);* he is a small olive-hued food fish of Europe and I only threw him into the plot because of his Greek-sounding name . . . and to see if you knew as much about fish as you do about *myths!!!!*"

There! That should sound sage enough to get your Dad's undivided attention and bring him back to the lesson at hand. Start with the Tarpon's scientific name, *Megalops atlantica.* "Atlantica" tells you right away that he is found on the East Coast of our country, the Atlantic Ocean, the Gulf of Mexico, and the Caribbean Sea. He is found on both coasts of Florida and occasionally strays as far north up the Atlantic as New Jersey. There have been reports from as far up as Nova Scotia, but don't count on taking him much beyond the Florida state line. He is far more common to the South, down through the Keys and up Florida's West Coast through the Gulf to Texas and down into Mexico. He is definitely a fish that prefers warm water. Even in Florida, when the winter turns the water coolish he retreats to deep water offshore.

Get out your Rapalas and Bucktails and try it. Go out to the grass flats, in areas where you might expect to take Trout (you'll catch a lot of them, too), and if you're lucky, and you most likely will be, you'll see Tarpon "rolling," sometimes literally schools of them all through the flats. Cast out and hold on. When they hit in the shallow water, they spend most of the time in the air, shaking their heads and making things spectacularly tough. Then they will run straight out to sea, zipping along for perhaps two hundred yards before they take to the air once again. You will be using light tackle when fishing like this, which is why all the fun and why I like it the best. Fly-fishing down on the Keys is perhaps the best way to take them of all (because of the winds you're apt to encounter you need to be *good* with the rod). You'll need a competent guide, who will pole his small boat out over the flats and along channels where, like

Look for the picture of a jumping Tarpon on page 130.

the plugging or spinning above, you will see the fish roll. Cast a few feet ahead of the direction they are moving. You need to give the saltwater streamer fly a fairly good action. Pause for a moment, young teacher of dads, and pity your tutor (that's me). Of all the fish in this book, perhaps it's the Tarpon I know best. I have caught many, many times my fair share—and released every one that I've caught. I was even a guide for a while down in Boca Grande Pass. I have fished them all over their range, and yet I find them the most difficult of all fish to discuss. Perhaps it's because I feel in a way that they should have their own book. The best way to continue may be to tell a few stories about Tarpon. I mean really true stories, not myths. Perhaps you will pick up a few clues as to the nature of the way of the Tarpon.

The first Tarpon I met was a wee guy about the size of a Sardine. I suppose I should clarify and say the *first Tarpons,* for there were literally thousands of them. My Dad and I had been using a seine (a long net) to capture Sardines for bait. I was about seven or eight and perfectly capable of handling my end of the job, which was to stand on the beach, holding one end of the net (which was attached to a broomstick) while my Dad waded out up to his waist (over my head) to encircle a school of Sardines. He would then work in to the shore about thirty feet from where I was standing and presto! we'd have a net full of bait.

This one time, however, we captured at least a thousand small Tarpon. To be perfectly honest, I couldn't tell the difference, but my father quickly ran back into the water and emptied the net. He showed me one of the small fish that had been stranded high on the beach. He pointed out the distinctive dorsal fin with the thread. "Those Tarpon we'll save until you are big enough to handle them." I thought he was mad—a little Minnow like that.

That evening, a couple of friends of my Dad's dropped by for a visit and the talk turned to the Tarpon. My Dad mentioned the haul we had made that very morning. It was the first time that I remember hearing stories about Tarpon. Somebody told a story about a lady who had gone fishing off Point of Rocks, a favored place for catching small Snapper. She was using a handline, which from the story I heard should have been called a toeline, for that's where she'd tied it, while she took a snooze in the sun. As you have probably guessed already, a Tarpon of considerable size came along and took off with her line and her toe. I'm not sure that it's true. I certainly hope that it's not, but one of the guys there made the remark that, because it was a Tarpon, "a toe might have been worth it." I never found out whether or not he loved Tarpon that much or the lady that little. I had nightmares for quite a long time after that, about fish that looked like Sardines but grew to size adequate to take off a toe. I resolved that I'd catch one, but not with a handline tied to my toe or anything else that I valued.

A Story About Tarpon

The first Tarpon I almost caught:

was when I was out fishing for Mackerel off the bridge. At the time I carried (in addition to the outfit that I used to whip up the Mackerel) an old split-bamboo "deepsea" rod with an old clanky Ocean City reel mounted on it. It was half-loaded with half-rotten line of about 120 pounds of test. I had traded Joey Williams a Daisy air rifle for it. (We had each gotten the worst of the bargain.) At any rate, my usual procedure was to run down under the bridge when I first arrived and quickly catch a Pinfish or two, which feat is no problem at all down in these waters. I'd rush up to the bridge and bait the big rod with a Pinfish and somehow or other manage to get it out into the channel, where I hoped to catch a big Shark or a Grouper.

But, secretly, deep down inside I wished for a Tarpon. This went on for a couple of weeks and all I managed to catch were a few rather small Stingrays, stingarees as we called them. (I wasn't impressed with deepsea fishing at all.) But, as I have said in some of the stories before, "I never give up" and so, as I hoped, it finally happened. A Tarpon passing through took the bait. I grabbed up the rod as he jumped. He came back to the water and ran just a few feet and jumped once again. He must have seen what was holding him and had a good laugh, and probably wished it had been tied to my toe. He gave a good pull on the run and, as rotten luck will have rotten line, the whole thing fell apart and he was gone. I tried to trade the outfit back for my rifle, but my luck was still running bad and that one got away too.

The first Tarpon I did catch:

was down off the "Everglades," town name of Marco. My Dad had taken us there to catch spotted Sea Trout, although I suspect, looking back, he had something else in mind. After all, we could take all the Trout that we wanted right out in front of our house. Maybe he did it because I kept talking about the Tarpon that had busted my line (incidentally, a line that became progressively stronger, and ditto the fish, every time I would tell the tale). Anyway, we rented a boat and moved out to some small islands of mangrove near the flats where there were a couple of good channels nearby. My Dad had suggested that we use plugs. They had a white body and red head, and I don't remember the name. They were just plugs. The fishing

I had the Tarpon completely under control!

was slow and I made a few comments to that effect. I even suggested that the plugs were too large for Trout.

I guess it was about then that it happened, about fifteen feet from the boat, so fast I wasn't prepared. I admit I came close to a panic. Out of the water came a Tarpon, straight for the boat. He missed us by inches. Then it began: mad rushes and jumping and water and spray all over the place. But I had him under control; I could hear his gill plates rattle as he'd come up shaking his head, and then he started off on a straight and strong run away from us.

"Just keep up pressure; not too heavy, son; let him run." I couldn't answer my father, I was speechless with excitement and remained that way right to the end, which came after what seemed like a couple of hours.

The fish wasn't huge for a Tarpon, sixty pounds more or less. But wait until it happens to you or your Dad. You'll think it's the biggest thing you've ever seen. My Dad slid the fish up to the boat and held him there with a small gaff through the lower jaw. He worked the treble hooks free and let the Tarpon go. I hope you will understand how much I wanted that fish, to take him home and show off. I didn't come right out and say it. I just hinted around.

"Sure would have liked for Mom to have seen that there Tarpon."

"Yes sir," he said, "she sure would have admired him. But the fact is, I think she'll admire you more."

"But she won't really know," I tried lamely.

"Oh, but she will! You're a fisherman now, son. She'll believe, and she will know." I guess then, you might say, that the reason I love Tarpon is he is the fish that made a fisherman you can believe out of me. Thinking back now, I guess he might have been eighty-some pounds. After all you never know for sure when you let them go.

Tarpon are not at all fit for the table, so let your fish go when you catch one. The memory will be your everlasting reward as you watch one of the great fighting fish of this world swimming proudly away. After all, he's a fish that almost made it to Mars.

Dolphin

If you are a smart teacher, and I am quite sure that you are, you will know right away that when a fisherman speaks of the Dolphin he speaks not of those small whales that are mammals but of fish that are *fish*.

One quite easy way to explain to your Dad the difference between the Dolphin the *fish* and the Dolphin or Porpoise the *mammal* is to ask him if he knows who Flipper is.

"Who is Flipper?" you ask. He probably knows. If not tell him that Flipper is the "Dolphin," a porpoise and mammal, a bright TV star the whole cast thinks they can talk to. (Oh well; and why not?) This kind of Dolphin can be taught to jump through a hoop and play with a ball (which, according to some, makes him as smart as we are). But now take a good look at his color.

"What color?" you ask. "He looks just dull brown or blah gray or ecch black." In other words, a bright mind and dull body.

Now look at the picture of the Dolphin the *fish,* and explain that you can't teach him to jump through a hoop or play with a ball, and no one I know believes that he can talk. But without doubt he's the most colorful fish in the sea: vivid blue greens and touches of purple and yellow, spotted and dotted, edged here and there with traces of gold and/or red, dark vertical bars that appear and disappear as he swims—in short, a peacock-colorful body and a fish brain.

I don't mean that crack about a "fish brain" to be in the least bit demeaning. As a matter of fact, I am in love with this fish and am glad for his brain. After all if he had a brain like his namesake the mammal, all we would have is a more colorful trick as he jumped through a hoop.

The Dolphin is known in some places as the Dorado. Most fishermen would know him by either good name. Scientists refer to

I've drawn this colorful, middle-weight champ for you on page 163.

him as *Coryphaena hippurus.* Try that out on your Dad. "Gee! That old hippurus can jump!" If you wish to explain what *hippurus* means, go ahead and tell him it means, "Horse-like and decorated with flower petals." This may not be the best translation but I like it because it's absurdly romantic.

Dolphins are found worldwide in tropical and subtropical seas. They are an oceanic species that love the Deep Blue. They are found up and down the entire East Coast of our country, but it is down in the southernmost parts that you are most apt to find them. When they do occasionally wander up north *in the summer,* they travel the Gulf Stream, which I suppose is a great way to go. It's a warm and beautiful current that moves along north about five knots an hour. It has its beginnings down in the Equatorial Current and then moves northward through the Caribbean into the Gulf of Mexico before racing through the Florida Straits and up the coast, where off New England it starts meandering for northern Europe, and there it mixes with and dies in the Labrador Current. (Thank heavens that Dolphin are at least smart enough not to go all the way. It would get pretty cold.) I am sure that there are fishermen up in New Jersey and New York who will say, "You're kidding. We never catch Dolphin up here." Well, tell them they could; but there is a stumbling block. They would have to travel a good many miles out to sea, all the way out to the Gulf Stream, which might be, at least, a hundred miles offshore. Florida got lucky again, for down there you can catch them within sight of the beach. Anywhere you are likely to find Sailfish and/or Marlin, you will also meet up with the Dolphin, which in a way shortchanges the fisherman. Dolphin are strictly a light-tackle fish. (And I have no reservation whatever in telling you that they are one of the fighters supreme.) Unfortunately, most fish that are caught are taken by fishermen out after Sailfish or Marlin, and the tackle they use is simply too heavy for best sport with Dolphin. Very few people go out just for the Dolphin. Most of the charter-boat captains will say that Dolphin are simply too scattered; the fishing's too slow or too dependent on luck. Well, now, that may be and then again it may not. I am one of the few who loves to go just for the Dolphin, with the proper matched tackle (light saltwater tackle, the twelve-pound test class). I'd pass up a "sail" for a colorful Dolphin. I think that they are stronger, pound for pound, just as spectacular, and on top of it all the best-eating fish in the sea.

If you have not eaten it up to now, try fresh Mahi-mahi, which is what Dolphin is called in Hawaii. Dolphin, as far as I am concerned, come in two sizes: the school size, from five to fifteen pounds, and the big ones, called bulls, that are common up to fifty pounds or better. The rod-and-reel record is 76 pounds. I am quite sure that they go as high as a hundred, and I myself fishing alone down off of Antigua in the West Indies took and released one that was almost six feet in length; I guessed that he weighed close to or better than 80 pounds. Dolphin love to hang out around "drift," anything that provides them a bit of shade. Look for patches of sargassum weed floating about, or a plank or perhaps a crate that's been dropped overboard. You can almost be sure that there'll be Dolphin under whatever. Tell your Dad to steer that way, troll by, and hold on; the strike of a Dolphin is spectacular.

Now, for "trade secrets" to pass on to Dad, a few hints that not many fishermen know.

I taught this to my Dad when I was quite young. We would go out near the Stream and I'd carry along the big Sunday paper complete with the comics. I'd open it up and spread a few sheets here and there over a pretty good area. We'd have either breakfast or lunch and clean all the gear and within an hour begin trolling, dragging the feathers up close and past the day's "news." (It may not be true, but I like to think that I once caught a Dolphin reading "Maggie and Jiggs".)

Other things to keep your eye out for are Sharks, particularly Sharks feeding on small Minnow-type fish or small Mackerel. Get as close to them as possible, and when you look down deep into the clear beautiful water don't be surprised to see a couple of big bull Dolphin cruising about, right with the Sharks. I've seen it so many times that I suppose there must be an "Odd Couple" play going on in the sea.

Tell your Dad that if you find a spot with a number of school Dolphin about, catch the first one and then leave him in the water, swimming freely about at the end of 25 to 35 feet of line; soon the entire school will come milling about and they'll stick around for awhile. That's the time to break out the light spinning outfits and the Bucktails or Rapalas and have a delicious fun time. I once did that from a rubber life raft, just drifting along with the Stream, casting a flyline with streamer attached. I don't believe I've ever had a more wonderful day. Dolphin of the West Coast are fished exactly the same, as they are in all waters I've been. Baja, again, is the place you should go. The Sea of Cortez, from Mulegé down to Cabo San Lucas, is loaded with Dolphin from late spring to the fall.

Dolphin will take almost any type of lure or rigged bait. They prefer everything trolled rather fast. My favorite lure is the *Knucklehead,* made by Sevenstrand, either in gold or in blue. Feathers and spoons and plugs of all types attract and take Dolphin, who are opportunistic feeders with voracious appetites.

By the way, speaking of appetites, I always keep one of the catch for the table and let the rest go. After all, a fifty-pound fish takes care of most any old table. I like to think that the rest are free to go roaming and perhaps looking for "news" or comics to read, like "Maggie and Jiggs," to show those drab "brainy" mammals that jump through the hoops who's smarter than who.

A Story About Dolphin

I guess I knew I was going out after Dolphin. I guess I even knew what they were, as no Florida boy would have confused them with Porpoise. But I sure didn't know what to expect. As I explained in the story about Tarpon, my deepsea experience to this point had been off a bridge.

You might even recall that old rod with the rotten line that I had traded an air rifle for. Well, you might as well get to know all about that old rod, as it figures pretty much in this story. And you also might as well know that even today, when I think of how I got took by my friend Joey Williams, I either laugh or get mad. I get mad when I think of the Tarpon and I laugh when I think of the Dolphin, so I guess in a way it was after all a pretty fair trade—or so it became.

After the Tarpon busted my line when I fished off the bridge, I got serious about fishing and tackle. I oiled up the reel and loaded it full with the cheapest and heaviest green line I could find on the shelf down at Tucker's, the tackle store that got all my trade. The rod was made of split bamboo and felt as if it weighed somewhere close to a pound. The butt or handle had been lathe-turned to look like an old spindle bed post, which was the smart style in those days. My guess would be that you could have bought one like it, brand new, right off of the rack, for less than two bucks. (I mention price only so you might have a good idea of its quality.) The reel seat was chrome over brass, and I know it was brass because half the chrome had flaked off. One guide was missing, which to me didn't seem totally bad, for three were still fixed firmly in place. I suppose that if I had any real objections at all it was that the rod had absolutely no bend, despite its intent and purpose. It was neither more nor less than a tapered broomstick, and I loved it, particularly so after I had finished it up with about ten gooey coats of orange shellac.

Anyway, my Dad had set up a deal with Capt. Frank, who ran a charter fishing-boat service at the foot of Main Street, out by the Chamber of Commerce, which was on the town's public pier. Capt.

Frank had the biggest and best boat of the whole fishing fleet. His was a forty-foot Chris Craft, complete with rust stains on the side and a line full of laundry, not to mention the smell of success. How he ever lived on her I'll never know.

But one thing he had aboard was first-class tackle and a wonderful knowledge of fish.

I guess, looking back, I might have been foolish to insist on using my own rod. But you must, I am sure, understand how I felt. After all, pride is a pretty loud noise in your ear when you are young, and besides I wanted to show Joey Williams what a wonderful trade I had made. In a way, I had it all well rehearsed. "Look here at this fish; reckon he goes two hundred pounds, soaking dry, an' you ain't got nuthin' yet with that ol' BB gun 'cept maybe a winder or two." Yes, sir, I went deepsea fishing well prepared for everythng except the Dolphin.

We went out early that morning, headed for maybe twenty or thirty miles off the beach. Because I didn't know any better and couldn't wait to get out to the Amberjack Reef, I put on a feather about five inches long and started to troll. I didn't really expect to catch any fish at the speed we were moving, but my Dad said I was right to try. "At least we know one thing for sure," he said, "and that is nobody ever caught anything without putting his line in the water."

I had the only feather aboard and, you might as well know, we were on our way to fish bait. We carried live Pinfish and Grunts, and we were sure to take some mighty big fish out by the reef. Capt. Frank always came in with Amberjack and sometimes some really big Kings, not to mention big Groupers and sometimes mighty big Sharks. Sharks, which he always brought back, were his best advertising. A big Hammerhead or Tiger Shark would always attract quite a crowd, mostly tourists that never paid much attention to the good-eating Groupers and Kings, but a Shark! My, they would line up and gawk; Capt. Frank could sometimes write a trip right then and there. I guess he was right, but still I'd made up my mind if we caught any big Hammerhead—at least if I did—I'd be letting them go. I've always liked Sharks for some reason still not clear to myself.

Anyway, I was really relaxed, my feet propped up on the transom. I might have dozed off for all of the action my feather provided. Capt. Frank spotted something floating about a half mile away. We were some ten miles off the beach. It was mighty peculiar, and we couldn't quite make it out, so we headed that way. So help me, it was a mattress out floating in the middle of the sea, grey and white ticking. We certainly all wondered where in the dickens a mattress might have come from. Perhaps from Old Mexico.

"Reckon it's any good?" I asked.

"Wouldn't reckon so," said my Dad.

And we all agreed that it was mighty waterlogged. "It's mighty waterlogged," said the Captain—and that's when the Dolphin came

After I caught the Dolphin I traded the rod back to Joey for my BB gun, sight unseen!

out of the sea and my heavy rod almost came out of my hands. Capt. Frank cut the engine and everybody started yelling instructions at once. I never saw such confusion. The only one with a sensible thought was the Dolphin; he went on a run and rampage like nothing I'd ever witnessed before. He started to sound and the

DOLPHIN • 147

line whizzed through the water, and the leather thumbstall on my reel really started to heat up. I could hardly keep up the pressure. Then he came out of the water and skyward again, twisting and turning on the way down, and then another mad dash that put a permanent set in my "broomstick." Well, not really permanent, because that's when the rod broke, right at the spindled bed-post of a butt. Talk about confusion. No matter how bad it had been to this point, now everything happened at once.

I sat there holding a rod butt and reel with line running out in a blur, and the broken tip of the rod banged around like a runaway yoyo and endangered everybody as it flew about out of control. I guess I was stunned for a minute or two, and then, looking down at what I was holding, I started to scream for everybody to get out of my way. I discarded the butt and the reel; I grabbed hold of the line with my hands and started to play the fish in a primitive fashion which, I can tell you, wasn't easy at all. With all the confusion and tangle, the reel rolled around on the deck, tripping me up a couple of times. But a half hour later I'd won. I had the huge Dolphin to gaff and aboard.

I've got to tell you that that boat was a mess; there was a hundred yards of tangled heavy green line all over everything . . . the Captain, my Dad, and my feet. We caught some really good fish on this trip, some Jack and good heavy Groupers, but nothing, of course, in the same league with my Dolphin. When we got home, Capt. Frank asked if he could hang my fish for a while on the rack in front of the boat. I suspect that he signed up quite a few charters as a result.

Joey turned green when I had him over to see my great fish. I told him how I had fixed up the rod and all that, and then I traded it back, sight unseen, for the rifle. I made him throw in an extra $1.50—and that's why I can laugh.

BAIT: An Aside

At the beginning of this book, I told you that we would not deal with the subject of bait (in the true sense of the word), that all our fishing would be with artificials only. Now we come to a point when we must deal with (in the true sense of the word) many of the larger gamefish that are traditionally taken on rigged bait. A rigged bait is any small fish or other bait such as Squid, etc., that has a hook embedded somewhere in its body and then is sewed up nice and neat so it will hold up when you troll.

In effect what we have done is create an "artificial" with the real thing. Understand, of course, that most of the big fish like Tuna, Marlin, and Sails will hit true artificials made out of wood, plastic, or feathers sometimes even better than they'll take the rigged bait. It is unfortunate, however, that because of their manner of taking the lure, it is almost impossible to hook them on hardware. A big Marlin will come up and strike a trolled bait or lure with his bill. His object

Study the pictures on the opposite page on how to rig baits so that you will be smarter than marlin.

is to stun his prey; after that he moves in (taking his time) to feed. The fisherman, knowing this, fools him by dropping the bait back, with his reel in free spool. The boat is stopped and everyone waits for the Marlin to move in and finish his meal. Obviously if the bait had been made out of plastic, the Marlin would simply assume that he'd made a mistake and struck something silly. He'd go swimming off looking for something more to his liking.

How to rig a "bait" fish.

2. Length of copper wire or heavy fish line "threaded" with a long needle through the head of the bait. Make sure it passes through the eye of the hook.

leader

1. Cut a small vent here, remove the bait's entrails and insert leader and hook up to the mouth. If your bait is a very scaly fish, such as a mullet, you will get better action if you scale him. Some fishermen de-backbone the bait, which also helps the action. You can buy a de-boner at your tackle store. It looks like this:

It is inserted through the mouth or top of the head of the bait, and over the backbone. A twist, and the bone is removed.

3. Wrap the mouth tightly closed with the soft wire or line. Tie it off and you are ready to troll as soon as you have put on a swivel and attached same to your line.

How to rig a "bait" squid

leader

After you've rigged your bait, attach swivel to leader.

small bottlecork   split shot

measure and tailor your rig to the length of your squid bait. Thread your leader through the cork and pinch on the split shot to hold it in place. Put your hook on at the distance you've measured. Thread your leader through the head of the squid, the body, and out through the tip of the tail (remember that squids travel tail first). Pull on your leader and force the cork up into the proper position, as shown. Put a swivel on the leader, attach it to your line, and you are ready to troll with a squid.

The Tuna

You know *who* may want Tuna "that taste good." As for me, because I am not fishing with cans on a shelf, I want only Tuna with good taste. In other words I want Tuna that appreciate artistry with rod and reel and flock to the show. Of course, be advised that most Tuna with good taste are often snide critics or take-charge kind of guys.

There are a number of species of TUNA, but Tuna Salad's not one, nor is a *Star Kist* or Charley. Now, never you mind if your Dad might happen to think so; just go get him a tunafish sandwich on whole-wheat, and, as he enjoys it, explain.

TUNA belong to the Mackerel family of fishes (just look at that forked Mackerel tail). A couple of the Tuna are truly *BIG GAMEFISH* while others are reasonably small. Of course, not so small that you will go rushing about with a Trout rod, for Tuna regardless of size are *extremely robust and strong.*

The largest and perhaps the most important (for fishermen) of all of the Tuna is the BLUEFIN; his scientific name is very "tunerish"-sounding indeed. He is called *Thunnus thynnus,* a name so odd that, if you go around yelling out to your Dad, you stand in danger of winding up with a cute little lisp. I think it is preferred, in this case, simply to shout: "A BLUEFIN IS ON . . . I thee him! I thay! I think!"

Let's set up the lesson on Tuna by discussing in detail just this one, the Bluefin. But first introduce Dad to a few of the others that, if he's lucky, he'll catch.

YELLOWFIN TUNA: *Thunnus albacares*. Worldwide, in tropical and sub-tropical seas, a possible 400 pounds (150 is more like the average).

BIGEYE TUNA: *Thunnus obesus*. About the same size and distribution as the Yellowfin. However he is not as frequently taken as is the Yellowfin or others within the same range. He is more important to the commercial fishing industry.

ALBACORE: *Thunnus alalunga*. This is the guy in the can that is labeled "white meat of tuna." (He's quite likely the guy that your Dad is munching on . . . if you made him the sandwich.) He is found in both the Atlantic and Pacific, but it's the Pacific that has the big edge. He is one of the most important gamefish off Southern California and south of there. He is one of the smaller Tuna; 69 pounds is the rod-and-reel record. Commercially Albacore have been taken off Hawaii up to 93 pounds.

BLACKFIN TUNA: *Thunnus atlanticus*. Found in the Tropical-Subtropical Atlantic, from Florida south. He is most common around the West Indies, a game little fighter and very good eating. He averages from 10 to 25 pounds. Occasionally you might take one closer to 40 .. . and if you are using very light tackle he'll give you a fit.

SKIPJACK and LITTLE TUNA: Distributed worldwide. These are generally picked up by fishermen after other species of gamefish. Because of their small size and the accidental quality of capture, we will discuss them in the chapter on *saltwater fun fish*.

Now back to the BLUEFIN and let's shake Dad up just a bit. First, as to size, no other Tuna comes even close to this giant fish; he is commonly caught at weights in excess of 400 or 500 pounds and reports suggest that he might reach 1,500 to 1,800 pounds. All I can say, if you were to hook one that big, is "Mercy—mercy, ten-four and out." I doubt if anything would be able to hold him, least of all me, as I value my back and only pair of arms, not to mention my time and my old family motto: "Life is too short, too sweet, and there are more catchable fish I'm waiting to meet." The world's record on rod and reel is 1,065 pounds. Bluefin are sometimes called Horse Mackerel and I'm sure that you have guessed why; it's only because of their size and great strength (they haven't got manes and never, but never, eat hay). If your Dad is just sitting and staring at the sandwich you made him, don't be alarmed; he's probably wondering after all that you've told him about size: "Why did you make his sandwich so small?"

Now for the practical side of the Tuna. They come in all sizes, and travel at times in tremendous schools. You and your Dad should have no trouble at all catching a few, at least some of the smaller ones. Every year, on both coasts, small Bluefin move in fairly close to the shore. If you are east in the summer, think of Long Island, for example: thousands of fishermen catch the smaller "school" fish there in July, August, September. They refer to the small Tuna as

The "old school" picture of these guys is on page 164.

THE TUNA • 151

"footballs." When you catch one, you'll see by the shape what they mean. As a rule, Tuna, like most "schooling fish," are of fairly uniform size in a school; they are graded as small, medium, or giant. "Small" means from about five pounds to a hundred, medium from that point to 250, anything over that is a giant. The smaller fish are far and away the more populous group and as such provide the best sport for most of us. The method of taking them is by trolling at a fast trolling speed, eight to ten knots, using feathers of various colors (preference as to color seems to vary from school to school or day to day). They will also hit Knucklehead lures and Rapalas. The ideal tackle for the smaller fish is twenty-pound class, a 2/0 or 3/0 reel loaded with line. Be advised that there is always a chance to hit a school of medium size and/or a few of the giants. Many of the charter-boat captains as a result go prepared with heavy tackle: 6/9 to 9/0 reels, and medium to heavy rods, 80- to 130-pound test line, and I think it a good rule that at least one of the outfits you troll be in that class. If it were my choice, I'd rig the heavy line with rigged Mackerel or Squid or a large Kona or Knucklehead lure.

There is a trick for laying out line when trolling for Tuna. I'm not sure that many fishermen know it and I suppose, as with every-thing, there are some who might disagree. Pay them no mind and go out and catch fish.

Here's how it is done.

Troll four lines as follows: two "flat" lines from the stern and two from the outriggers. I'm sure that your Dad knows what outriggers are. If not, tell him that they are long poles, usually of fiberglass or bamboo, mounted on either side of the boat. They are adjustable to a position that may be straight up or anything down to a line parallel to the water. Usually these are set for fishing at an angle of about 45°. This holds the two lines well away from the boat and, depend-ing on speed, certainly helps to skip a bait or a lure up to the surface. The outrigger lines should be fairly *long lines,* well behind the wake of the boat. They should be dressed at, as equal distances as possible, eighty to one hundred feet out. I consider the equal distance important, and I know of at least a few very successful Tuna fishermen that measure their lines to the inch. I suggest that one or both of these lines be your heavier outfit.

Now, for the flat lines (and this will surprise you), keep them *short* and keep them *flat* (down close to the deck or the transom, the back of the boat). I use clothspins for this; you will see what I mean and how I would rig when you study the sketch.

Now understand "short." It takes a bit of convincing to prove that it works. Your two flat lines should be trolled about fifteen feet back, about at the crest of the boat's second wake (some prefer to play it in even closer, right at the very first wake). Use feathers of about two to three ounces for this.

Start off with the following popular color choices: dark green and yellow on one, and red and white on the other. If the darker lure is

look at the diagram on the opposite page.

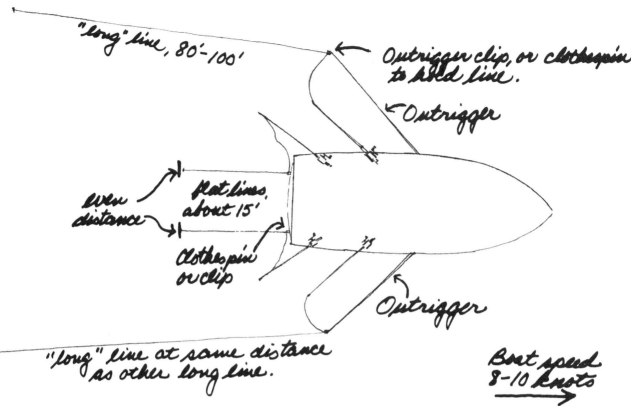

"long" line, 80'-100'

Outrigger clip, or clothespin to hold line.

← Outrigger

even distance

flat lines, about 15'

Clothespin or clip

Outrigger

"long" line at same distance as other long line.

Boat speed 8-10 knots →

hit first or more often, I would start changing the red and white for darker combinations: blues and greens, even some in browns and blacks. You will soon find what colors are most in demand. I will hazard a general guess (you can too!) though maybe you will want to keep it to yourself, until you take your Dad out fishing for school Tuna. Point to the "flat" line with the yellow-and-green feather and tell everyone within earshot that it will take the first fish. I call it my fishfinder rod, and I have found that it successfully takes the first fish about 60 percent of the time.

Most of the techniques for taking Tuna go well, as a rule, for all species. However there are times, with species other than Bluefin, that the fish prefer only long lines. You must experiment to find this out for yourself.

Most of the really giant Tuna are captured on rigged bait rather than lures. Sometimes the only way to take them is to drift fish, using live bait such as small Mackerel or Whiting or Cod. Usually drift-fishermen chum up their fish by dribbling in ground-up or cut-up Menhaden or Mossbunkers (they are the same fish).

I have stressed fishing for the smaller and medium-sized fish, because they are easily within reach of almost everyone and are delightful to catch. Running out just for the big ones entails slightly more work and expense, but it would be well worth your while if you are in the right place at the right time: off Block Island or around Nova Scotia or down in the Bahamas when they run.

THE TUNA • 153

Oddly enough some fish prefer great turbulence and white water; Bluefin and other Tuna definitely do. Most of them seem to have little fear of the boat *IF* the speed is held steady. The drive-shafts should be correctly aligned, and look out for nicks in the propellers (the boat should run smoothly, with a minimum of vibration). Many fishermen out there wonder why they are not catching fish while a neighbor pulls one after another out of the very same school. If you took a ride in each of their boats, I'd be willing to bet that you'd find a great deal of pleasure in the sound and the ride of the successful fisherman's boat; the unlucky guy's will rattle your teeth. Be kind and tell him to get it all straightened out. There are a lot of little tricks in almost all types of fishing, and probably more for the Tuna than anyone else. One of the things you might notice is that it seems that twin-engine fishing boats are slightly more successful at taking fish right in the wake than are single-screw boats. The reason is simple: the twin throws up a bigger, more mountainous wake than the single, and when I say these fish prefer turbulence that's what I mean. If you own or if you fish from a single-screw boat, you can help the situation a lot by dragging behind an old tire (in close to the stern) or anything else that might give you more white water behind.

If you feel silly doing something like this and are afraid that someone might laugh when you get back to the dock, simply tell them (with a straight face) that you were afraid that you might have a flat and so carried a spare. Now step back about fifteen feet and give him a lateral shot with a Tuna and say, "Here's a football for you." (Make sure that your receiver is not too close to the edge of the dock.)

Assume that by now he's stopped laughing (most of them do) and will probably ask some sensible questions.

Well, like for example: "How do you find Tuna out on such a big ocean?"

Tell him, "I put on the spare and went looking for Petrels." (Be careful to sound dignified and serious when you say this or you might get your football passed back to you.) Explain that Petrels are small birds that most people call "Mother Carey's chickens." They fly far out to sea and, as a rule stay low, close to the water. They look nothing at all like most of the Gulls, Terns, and other seabirds that you will meet. They are small, dark-colored birds that dart here and there; but they are experts at locating Tuna. If I saw some small dark birds playing around in the distance, that's where I'd head.

A Story About Tuna

In a way, I'm ashamed of this story, but I'll tell it anyway, because I'm also rather proud. I'll not cite my age because, if I did, I might be tempted to make myself a little bit younger, at least young enough to have an excuse and not feel at all guilty about what I had done. Of course you must understand that, if I had been older, no excuses would have been needed. I could simply say, as more mature people say, "I did what I did because I have a great deal of sense." Nobody with any wisdom and age to his or her credit would have held me accountable. As it was, I was at an in-between age where there is no excuse based on either extreme youth or maturity.

I threw one of my Dad's trolling rods overboard with a two-hundred-pound-plus Tuna attached.

My Dad and I went down to Bimini in the Bahamas with a couple of friends. We had gone with the idea of tackling Tuna or Marlin. Bimini was an ideal spot; it faced right to the Gulf Stream, which in those days was required or, at least, desired. As it turned out, we spent all our time fishing for Tuna and they were big. Beginning on Monday, we trolled with rigged Mullet bait and by Tuesday evening everybody but me had hooked up with fish but no one had been able to land one. They either had broken off or were attacked by the Sharks, who were everywhere and doing a pretty fancy butchering job on the Tuna. A couple of times we landed nothing but heads. It was much sadder than fun. The captain stood by with a rifle and shot up a number of Sharks, but the battle and the war both seemed to be lost; in a way, I was glad that I hadn't hooked up, and even, a couple of times, wished I was back on the dock catching Palometas (long-finned Pompano) and/or Jacks, both of which you could see hunting about, down deep in the clear and beautiful water. They were a great deal of fun, and I was at the age where I handled them with finesse. And I didn't worry about Sharks or half-eaten fish.

So here (with considerable courage) is the story about the first Bluefin Tuna I hooked.

It was on our third day trip, on Wednesday. We had left the dock at sunrise; the sea was exceptionally calm, "oil-slick smooth," as my father would say. The run to the "fishing grounds" was a short one as, down in these waters, every mile within sight was as good as the next one. I suppose we ran twenty minutes before we started to fish. My line with a freshly rigged Mullet was the first to go out. I was assigned the port outrigger, which was okay with me, as I had secret plans to be down below if a fish hit. It was truly my intention to let somebody else handle my rod should it be hit. I had no intention of feeding a fish to the Sharks. I was holding the rod as the mate ran my line up the outrigger pole.

The Tuna hit with a crack, before my line had reached half way to its mark. I was stuck fast to a mighty big fish and knew I had to go it alone. My attitude changed in a flash. I realized at once that I had been overly pessimistic for the past couple of days, because I had been left out of the fun. Well, now here it was and I "yahooed" at the top of my lungs. I was determined to be the first one aboard to bring in a big whole, uneaten Tuna to gaff.

All the shooting at Sharks, the two days gone by, had left me with a feeling for battle. This was to be the major campaign of the war. I thought like a Pershing, fought like Jackson at the battle of New Orleans; in my mind I was John Paul Jones and David Farragut rolled into one. But even with all of those strengths, the Gulf Stream became my Little Bighorn.

It was a bloody and one-sided battle, and I am the one who got bloodied.

All because of the chair. Back in those days we didn't have "fighting" chairs like you see on the boats of today. What we had were good, sturdy, honest mahogany desk chairs, painted white, gimbaled, and mounted on posts so that they'd swivel. I suppose, in a way, they were somewhat less torture out on the Gulf Stream than they were in an office, although I felt at the time that they were not. (I am sure there's many a man who's spent his life in an office on one of those chairs and who would gladly bring one along to the Stream to prove that I was wrong.) Anyway, I didn't "fit" in the chair (I was too small) and I didn't have shoes on, and that's how come I got bloodied and wound up losing the war.

The first thing to go was my seat (and I don't mean the chair). In a little less than an hour, I had cookie-sized blisters on both of my cheeks. I tried to hold myself firmly to avoid further damage, bracing my feet on the transom . . . so they were the next parts of me to sustain battle damage. I bruised all the toes on the right foot and pulled a cartilage deep in the heel of the left.

My arms were well past the stage of feeling like lead; they were deader than numb. My hands were locked with a death grip around the butt of the rod, and I pumped erratically. All the veins in my arms looked as if they'd pop any minute. I asked for some help and was advised (quite correctly) that I "could do it," words that ran all mumbled together and didn't impress me a bit. "Must do it!" "No one can help you, son, those are the rules": listening to all of the mumble and the sound of my own voice asking for help, I started praying for Sharks (they are never around when you desperately need them).

I fought. Oh, how I fought! I was going to win, had to win. I could hear more mumbles: "Looks like he's turned. Keep pumping, son." "I can see him, there, over there."

That's when the battle was lost. The big Tuna turned from the boat and went into a dive straight down and out. I was pulled against buckling knees, painfully sliding just enough so that the

I let the rod go, because of my blisters!

blisters both broke and started to bleed. The sun seemed to flash in great bright explosions on the wrong side of my eyes, turning everything red, and my body gave up the battle. My hands unlocked and let the rod go. And it went—after the Tuna.

Now you know why I'm always a little ashamed when I tell this "first Tuna" story. And it's not because I lost the fish or the rod or the war; it's because I had to mention the blisters I got on my seat.

Billfish

Take up weight-lifting! Play catch with a medicine ball and run twenty miles every day! Eat lots of fish! Go to bed early and dream. You're going to need all the help you can get.

First ask your Dad, "What's a Marlin?" (Don't be surprised if he knows.) Of course if he says, "A magician in King Arthur's court," you have your work cut out for you. (Don't give up hope; you might be able to learn something about King Arthur.) Go about it this way. Ask your Dad what's so special about King Arthur (as if you didn't know). Your Dad will start to explain, about strength and endurance, and great noble deeds; about Excalibur, Arthur's sword. That's the opening that you'll wait for and when it comes, just say, "Aha! You *DO* know all about Marlin. The great noble fish with the sword."

Congratulations; you've probably hooked your Dad good with that one. Now reel him in and explain all about Marlin and the other great "billfish," which is the name of fish that sport a long upper jaw shaped like a sword or a "bill." Introduce them to Dad.

THE BILLFISH (there are quite a few):
ATLANTIC SAILFISH *Istiophorus platyperus*
PACIFIC SAILFISH
WHITE MARLIN *Istiophorus tetrapturus albidus*
STRIPED MARLIN *Istiophorus tetrapturus audax*
BLACK MARLIN *Istiophorus tetrapturus makaira indica*
BLUE MARLIN *Istiophorus tetrapturus makaira nigricans*
ATLANTIC SPEARFISH   *Tetrapturus belone* (shortbill)
                       Tetrapturus pfluegeri (longbill)
PACIFIC SPEARFISH *Tetrapturus angustirostris* (shortbill)
BROADBILL *Xiphias gladius*

The pictures of these big fellows take up pages 165 – 166.

Now have your Dad sit in a chair. Make sure that he's comfortable and very relaxed. Have him close his eyes and tell him to picture indigo blue seas, turning to purple in unfathomable depths . . . and now, swimming by, a great fish that weighs half a ton, fifteen feet long, with a sword for a nose. The fish gathers up speed: 20, 30, 40, 50 plus miles per hour. Up he comes now at 60, straight from the foot of the undersea mountain, the home of the deep-dwelling, great, giant Squid, up through the roof of the ocean, throwing sheets of white water and spray and, just for a moment, you see iridescent colors of blue like that found in rare butterfly wings, so brilliant that in contrast the rich indigo sea turns to gray. And then he is gone with a splash that your Dad can only imagine. When his eyes open, study your Dad for a moment. Just decide whether he's peaceful and calm or excited; no two dads react just alike to the vision. I remember my own, for example, his eyes kind of googled and he acted a little bit nervous.

Calm him down, if need be, by keeping the rest of his lesson quite simple. Don't make the mistake that I made, when I yelled right in the middle of my father's dream of the Marlin: "I'VE GOT ONE!!! THERE HE BROACHES!! STRAP ME IN!! BACK THE BOAT DOWN!" That is, as you might have guessed, what goggled his eyes . . . I had a heck of a time calming him down.

For scientists, the study of Billfish often gets rather complicated. Often the students of this superfamily of fishes disagree about such fine points as whether or not certain fish found in our two major oceans are in fact the same fish or just closely related yet distinctly different species. Fortunately, fishermen can still be students of all the Billfish and not give a darn about minor and barely detectable differences, like the number of scales or the twist of the lateral line.

Take the Sailfish as an example. They are found in both the Atlantic and the Pacific. Think of them as exactly the same, with only one difference that might matter at all to a fisherman, and that is their relative size. The Sailfish in the Pacific grows to a much larger size. Remember that size differences are quite common to many species of fish found in different parts of even the same sea. Even the Atlantic Sailfish are generally larger in the Gulf of Mexico than those that are taken off Palm Beach in the Atlantic proper. The average size of the Atlantic Sailfish is 40 to 50 pounds. He is a "light tackle" fish in every respect. A 20-pound test outfit is just about right.

You might explain to your Dad that there is a great spread indeed of size and weight between different species of Billfish. The little Atlantic Sailfish is one of the smallest (141 pounds is the largest recorded on rod and reel). The mighty Black or Blue Marlins may reach weights in excess of 2,000 pounds, but the rod-and-reel record for a Black was a fish that weighed 1,560 pounds (he was caught off Peru). The Pacific Sailfish reaches at least twice the weight of the Atlantic. The average here would be closer to 100 pounds.

The smallest of the Marlins is the White Marlin, ten pounds heavier than the Atlantic Sailfish, on the average, but a much stronger fighter. He is one of the great acrobats of the sea; when hooked, he seems to be constantly up in the air trying new tricks. He is found in the Atlantic only, and if you live on that coast anywhere from New England down through the South and into the Gulf of Mexico, you have somebody very special to brag about. Remember, because of his rather small size he's like the Sail, a light tackle fish (the same tackle will do for them both).

Now, moving up a notch in size, introduce to your Dad Mr. Striped Marlin, a fish that the Pacific Coast can brag about. He's almost as good an acrobat as the White; some claim he's better. I hope that someday you can decide that for yourself. I personally have my own preference, but out of loyalty to Nebraska, because they have neither, I'm not going to say.

The largest Striped Marlin taken on rod and reel was, I believe, listed at 483 pounds. It was taken off Chile, where the average is probably closer to 200 pounds. In waters closer to home on our West Coast, we must travel back down into Baja California and the Sea of Cortez. (Actually we don't have to; Striped Marlin are taken off Southern California, but the quality of fishing is poor and quite slow by comparison to the Sea of Cortez.) Striped Marlin arrive in that lower Gulf about April, hanging around through the summer at least until August. At the height of the season in the Sea of Cortez you'll have more hookups than you can handle. The Striped Marlin is far and away the most numerous in terms of the number of Marlin that are caught, a result in large part, I am sure, of the fact that this species of Marlin is found generally much closer in to shore.

Now for a really big jump in size: Meet the Black Marlin. Perhaps he's the fish of your father's great Marlin dream. He is the Muhammad Ali of all time, graceful yet strong as a bull. He doesn't jump as often as the White or the Striped, but when he does the only question you'll ponder is IF the ocean is big enough to hold him when he comes down. As of now, he is the heavyweight champ of the Billfish taken by rod and reel: 1,560 pounds caught off Peru. (To be honest, tell Dad that Blue Marlin grow to a slightly larger size and that, in fact, there was a Blue monster caught that weighed 1,805 pounds; but it's not considered the record because the rod was handled by more than one person. Let that be a lesson: if you are ever hooked to a record, DO IT YOURSELF.) The Black Marlin is reported by commercial fishermen to reach a weight of close to 2,000 pounds, and the Blue gets to 500 pounds more than that. Indeed, there are records yet to be set; go out and do it!

If you are after Black Marlin, you'll fish the Pacific or Indian Oceans, which is where they live. Technically, they have been taken in the Atlantic also, but, certainly as far as we know, not as a rule, though I believe that we will find more in the future, perhaps a great many more than scientists at the moment would think. Atlantic reports of the Black all place him down off the Cape of Good Hope, the southernmost tip of the African continent. If you ever have a chance to study a map of the floor of the Atlantic, look very closely at this area. You will see the Agulhas Plateau and its basin and the current by the same name that moves sort of counterclockwise at the tip of the Cape. I guess if I were a Great Black, knowing I had absolutely no enemies that lived in the sea—even Jaws of Hollywood fame wouldn't be a match for me, because I could swim twice as fast, if nothing else, and if I ever gave him a jab at full speed with my sword he'd be a pretty sick Shark for awhile. After all, with my sword I can pierce nearly four inches of steel or close to two feet of cured and very hard wood, like a ship's ribs made of oak. Yes, I think if I were a Great Black, I'd be bold and adventuresome and ride a good current up north, like the Benguela Current that moves up the west coast of Africa and into the South Atlantic "horse latitudes" at the Tropic of Capricorn, a region of light and slow shifting breezes, with air as bright and as fresh as any on Earth. I'd find plenty of food for my trip, like juicy Bonito and Tuna and Dolphin. But I guess you'd just have to wait to find out if and how far I as a Black Marlin might have penetrated another great ocean. For now, tell your Dad if he'd like to catch me to go down to Panama West or out to Australia.

Explain to your Dad that everyone won't get to go and catch Marlin, at least not the Black, but it's a dream you can surely work up to. And like the advice you gave Dad about the Atlantic Salmon, "If you never have a chance to go fishing for such a magnificent fish, you are richer by far just knowing about them."

ATLANTIC AND PACIFIC BLUE MARLIN:

As I might have implied, if you and your Dad want to go out and catch Marlin, your best bet would be the STRIPED MARLIN down in the Sea of Cortez. Now the second best bet might well be the BLUE, this despite the fact that he is probably the least common of all the Marlins. But look at his range, temperate and tropical seas all over the world, the Atlantic, the Pacific, the Caribbean, the Gulf of Mexico: in other words, you might find him surprisingly close to some place at home, in the Atlantic off North Carolina, and all points immediately south. The Bahamas, not far from the Florida shores or the Florida Straits, north of Cuba (where, at this writing, I suggest you don't go ashore for some cigars for your Dad). Just run up the Gulf toward old New Orleans, and, if you wish, even to Texas and then down the Mexican coast through the Yucatan Channel. Or you might try Bermuda or Puerto Rico or the Virgin Islands or anywhere through the West Indies. If you are on the West Coast of our country, you might try Baja again (although the great Blues are quite rare that far up north). The chances are good that you might take a Blue if you go to Hawaii (to look at the flowers) or down to Tahiti (which isn't all bad, though it's not close to home).

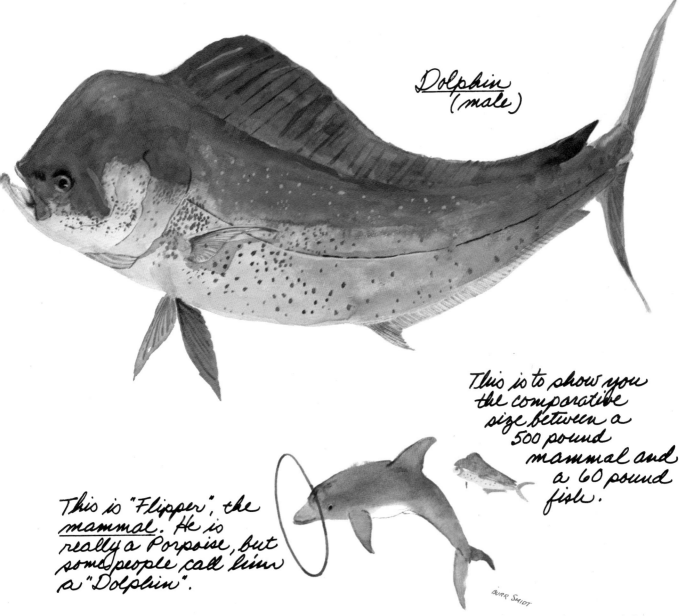

This is a sketch of a female Dolphin. You can tell she's a lady by the shape of her head. She wears the same pretty colors as poppa.

Dolphin (male)

This is to show you the comparative size between a 500 pound mammal and a 60 pound fish.

This is "Flipper", the mammal. He is really a Porpoise, but some people call him a "Dolphin".

BURR SMIDT

163

A few of the more common Tunas

Yellowfin Tuna — sometimes called "Allison" Tuna.

Skipjack Tuna
You might in some places hear him called "Oceanic Bonito".

Albacore or "Longfin"

This is the Giant Blue — fin Tuna — alias "Horse mackerel".

Blackfin Tuna
This guy gives you a good idea why it call the small Tunas "footballs".

164

Sailfish

Striped Marlin

165

Broadbill or Swordfish

BURR SMIDT

Typical Spearfish

166

But, as you can see, there's a very good chance that you won't have to travel as far to take a great Blue as you would to take a great Black.

I think you should suggest to your Dad that whether travel is or is not in your plans, you'd still go for the Blue just for his fight, which, coupled with size, is the best of them all. He is one of the fastest, can jump with the best, and is as strong as a runaway freight or the Black.

One of the reasons that I'd suspect that the Blue Marlin seems to be the least common of all these great fish is that he is the most "Oceanic." It might be of interest to know that though I refer to the Great Blue Marlin as "he," almost all of the truly *big* fish are "she."

Another species of Billfish is occasionally taken, so rare that they are not even classified by the International Gamefish Association, the group that keeps all the records and sets all the rules.

These fish are the *SPEARFISH:*

The Atlantic Longbill SPEARFISH *Tetrapturus pfluegeri*
The Pacific Shortbill SPEARFISH *Tetrapturus angustirostris*
and the Mediterranean Shortbill SPEARFISH *Tetrapturus belone*

None of them reach any great size, generally averaging less than forty pounds. They look as if they were a cross between Sailfish and Marlin (they're not), but maybe *they* think so and are ashamed to come in close to the shore. (I certainly wish they'd be proud!) Of all the Billfish, these are the *most* oceanic, more so in a way than even the Blue, who once in a while comes in toward shore to see what's going on. Spearfish apparently couldn't care less. Study the sketch of the Spearfish, just in case you or your Dad might catch one and the Captain tries to tell you that it's a "White" with a problem or a "Sail" that got caught in a storm. Just turn to your Dad and say, "I believe it's a *Tetrapturus pfluegeri* or perhaps a *Tetrapturus angustirostris* or a *Tetrapturus belone.*" If you play your cards right (don't get too cocky!), the Captain will give you a couple of hours more fishing. (Just show him this book.)

Now comes the time to teach your Dad about a fish that many fishermen consider the best. Even writers who write about fish generally open with some grandiose statement, like, for example: "The noblest fish of them all" or "The great gladiator, King of the Seas," and so forth. They are talking about the Broadbill or Swordfish (either name is okay).

Well, he may be all that they say but you couldn't prove it by me. "Ha!" you will say, "that means that you ain't never caught one!" Despite your appalling use of our language, I have to admit you are right. I have not. But I have been aboard a couple of times when they have been baited and caught and, having seen at firsthand some of the action provided, I'd be dumb as a writer not to start off playing it safe.

These fish are more than "just" fish. They are a challenge of unparalleled measure for anyone who fishes the sea. There, how is that? "That ought to hold them," you say. Well, I certainly hope you are right, for, if so, it's one of the very few things in this world that could. Let's start off by telling your Dad some of the negative things about the BROADBILL.

1. They don't grow quite as large as the Blue or the Black Marlin (at least as far as we know; but they might). Poor little fellows. The largest one caught to date was caught by Lou Marron off Chile, and it weighed 1,182 pounds.

2. They are mean. They use their swords much more than the other species of Billfish. They use them on Sharks (which isn't too bad), and they sometimes stick Whales (which isn't too good). They also are known to ram boats and great ships (which definitely is not encouarged by admirals any place in the world).

3. They are hard as the dickens to bait and to hook; believe it or not, despite the fact that they are mean they are also painfully shy. As you might have found out from dealing with a wide range of people, whenever you meet someone who's mean and, on top of that, shy, you have a big wad of trouble.

I guess, when you get right down to it, most of the above aren't really negatives (at least when you are dealing with fish). I was just being picky and I know that you know the reason for that (but I'll catch a Broadbill . . . some day).

On the positive side: Let's teach Dad what we know about the Broadbill. Let's start with the name, which implies quite correctly that this fish has a broad sword, *much* broader than any other Billfish. Though his name doesn't imply that his bill or his sword is longer than those sported by his cousins, it is, and considerably so. I guess if I had been in charge of passing out names I'd have called him The Longer Broader Billsworded Broadfish, which in itself is good proof of our luck, that I wasn't around passing out names. Anyway, good ole what's his name is found worldwide in all warm and temperate seas. (This puts him in range of fishermen on both coasts of our country.) We have areas in both the Atlantic and the Pacific that are renowned as "swordfishing" centers. On the Atlantic, one such area that comes quickly to mind is Block Island off Rhode Island. It is even suspected that large number of Broadbill winter deep, very deep, off the continental shelf directly off Block Island and Long Island as well. In the Pacific off Southern California and the Island of Catalina we also have large populations of this kind of trouble.

It certainly sounds easy: just hop in a boat, run out to the Island, catch a thousand-pound fish, and run home for lunch. We will find out as we go along why this isn't so.

Let's start with the Swordfish's eye. If you ever have a chance to stare at one, you'll get a chill. At least I can say that I do. Their eyes are immense (proportionally so). Very large eyes in a fish suggest, as a rule, that we are dealing with one who's at home in the darks of the deep—and, believe me, I don't mean just a few hundred feet, I am talking of *great* depth, at least a few thousand feet. Broadbills have been photographed down to a depth of about 3,300 feet. I am quick to suppose that their limits must be far greater than that. At any rate, it's too deep to fish. (You'd need a few hundred pounds of lead weight and a couple of miles of line just to get down, not to mention some kind of a very strong derrick on deck just to get up; and think how mad you would get if a Crab stole your bait . . . it just wouldn't work out at all.) Fortunately for us, Broadbill come up once in awhile to relax and bask in the sun on the surface. This is the situation that we look for; actually we "hunt" for. That is precisely what we do when we go after Broadbill, we hunt. The procedure is to run the boat well offshore where it's deep and the water is "blue water" blue. Then someone is sent high aloft as a lookout; some sportsfishing boats have towers or masts built just for this purpose. The lookout should have a good view over a couple of miles in any direction. Broadbill are quite easy to spot when they are sunning or swimming about on the surface. The high dorsal fin and sickle-shaped tail give them away (both are stuck high in the air).

Here is a picture of what a Broadbill looks like when he is out soaking up the sun.

At this point, now that we know who it is waving his fins, we'll pretend that it's a mile over there to the east. I suggest we pretend, because I'm quite sure you're not out in a boat looking at the fins of a Swordfish (nobody reads when out looking for Broadbill). My guess would be that you and your Dad are stretched out on the living room floor in front of a fire and you are teaching him tricks. So pretend you are out after a Broadbill and tell him precisely what it is he must do if he wants to catch that great fish over there. (If you are a good pretender, you can point.)

We've had our equipment ready all morning; for bait, a fresh-rigged large Squid or perhaps a Bonito; even a football-sized Tuna is good. Our bait is attached to the leader and line and rests ready for use in the bait box on a good chunk of ice; our great heavy outfit stands ready in the rod holder. The lookout yells, "There's a fish . . . THERE'S A FISH . . ." (Lookouts get very excited at times like this.) Perhaps you are excited yourself. You climb up the tower with your eagle eyes working like mad and there, sure enough, less than one mile away, due east, you see the fins. Maybe at first you'll think it's just a couple of big Mako Sharks. But . . . *HEY!* That fin to the rear is too high and too thin for a Shark. You realize, of course, that it must be a Broadbill.

You scramble down to get everything ready for action. First thing you do is attach your Dad's harness so that he can put his back and shoulders into the fight. (He'll need all the help he can get.) Now the boat maneuvers with a great deal of caution as you close to a few hundred yards from the fish. The slightest splash or unwanted commotion will wake the giant Broadbill in a moment and he'll dive, disappear back into the depths.

Now you drop Dad's bait over the stern and begin to pay out the line. You know that you need a very long line for the troll, since you won't be approaching too closely. When you have about 175 to 200 yards of line trailing behind, you stop and hold the line with your hand. You call out to Dad to pay out more line—60 to 70 feet more. This you can let trail in a loop in the water. Quickly explain to your Dad why you have had him do this. It's because, if the fish strikes with his bill, you quickly release the line to the bait that you have been holding and with that extra line from your Dad the bait will drop back, like a free-swimming fish that's been struck. You yell to the captain to kick the boat into neutral and to stand by. (Most swordfishing-boat captains won't have to be told; they know what to do. If this wasn't pretend, I'd suggest that you shut up and just let your nerves tingle.) Now comes the wait. A Swordfish takes plenty of time. If he picks up the bait, he'll start to move off at a strong, steady, and usually slow pace. If he's been hooked on the strike, which you, of course, will hope is the way that it happens, you follow the same nervous procedure. You wait and keep paying out line. When you are sure the fish has indeed taken and is moving off, perhaps starting to pick up some speed, yell to the captain, "Let's strike." He'll know what you mean. He'll kick the gears into forward and give her the gun. At the same time have your Dad bring his rod up sharply a number of times. You must really work to set that big hook firmly. Now, hold on to your Dad's hat. He'll have his hands full and won't be able to do anything else but pump and try to hold on for perhaps a couple of hours. If I were you, I think I'd go down below and make myself a peanut butter sandwich to stick all my nerves back together.

Well, pretend time is over. Now tell your Dad that in reality it's very hard to get Broadbills to strike when they are sunning on the surface. I'm darned if I know why. I would guess that, for whatever reason, they don't feed when they sun, and you will be one of the chosen handful of fishermen if you are lucky enough to connect just once in awhile.

All of which means I am not one of the chosen. As you said yourself, ''I ain't never caught one''—as yet.

A Story About Billfish

It's not very often that one gets to go out and catch a Billfish. This is particularly true when one is both little and young. When I was young it was even more true. For one thing, big-game fishing tackle was in its infancy just about the time that I was. Most of the reels of that period had no brakes and no drags and, as everyone knows, neither do fish. This made it quite hard on the fisherman when he went out to tackle a big one. All one had to work with in those days was a leather thumbstall on the reel over the spool, a crude kind of brake (naturally one had a thumb with which to apply pressure). It was a touch-and-go method of fishing, even for grownups, who, as a rule, had very big thumbs.

Catching a large fish that sported a bill was a dream that I'm sure most Florida boys shared; many of us, of course, had seen the big fish as they broached or finned on the surface out on the sea. My dream didn't come true until I was considerably older and owned my own boat, "Arvie." Reels by that time were handsome affairs designed to save thumbs. (Which was really smart thinking, as most fishermen only had one thumb in reserve.)

My first Billfish actually came as a *pair* of Sailfish, and I can tell you that none of my dreams had quite prepared me for that. Should it happen again exactly the way that it did the first time, and despite all the practice I've had since, I'm sure that I'd still wind up in a tangle of thumbs.

There's a side to this story that has to do with a contest, and every time I think about it I burst out laughing aloud. Every year, off Palm Beach, Florida, they hold one of the grand tournaments of fishing, the Sailfish Derby. Top sportsmen from all over the world gather to compete. It is quite an affair.

Personally I am not into competitive fishing but I do love to stand off to one side and enjoy the fun. On the occasion of this story, I inadvertently found myself in the middle of a fierce contest, with which I had nothing to do.

I was crossing over to Bimini (just for the trip). I was all by myself on my 29-footer "Arvie." As it turned out, it was the third day of the Sailfish Derby. As I approached the edge of the Gulf Stream I found myself "mingling" with a number of the beautiful boats from the tournament fleet; there must have been ten or fifteen within sight. One of the most beautiful was so close that I could make out her name, "Pursuit." Being friendly as well as interested in how they were doing, I called "Pursuit" on the radio.

"How's it going, Captain?" I asked.

"Pretty darn slow," he replied. "Hasn't been a fish taken in the first two days of the contest."

"Well, that's pretty bad," said I.

"Yeah, first year we've had this kind of a bust!" he said sadly.

"Well," I offered, "maybe things will improve. Anyway, good luck, Captain, and keep those lines tight! Arvie clear with Pursuit."

I decided, as I finished the conversation, that I might as well waste some time, too. I put out a couple of lines, rigged with *Knucklehead* lures. Actually I hoped I might pick up a Dolphin as I crossed through the Stream. I could still make out the name of "Pursuit" when both my lines went off at once. Up they came and out of the water, a pair of beautiful Sailfish, crossing and forming an X right at my stern. I can truthfully tell you that I have never seen anything quite as grand and heart-stopping in all my life.

But of course it's what happened next that I shall always remember. "Confusion" is too mild a word, "chaos" too bland. If you think strange crazy thoughts of the kind you sometimes have in a dream, you might, for a moment, be able to place yourself there on my boat. Think of the soles of your shoes covered with well-chewed, pink bubblegum and the floor covered with feathers and buckets and you stumble around, clutching handfuls of buttered spaghetti, and sirens are screaming. Radio voices scream too: *"Pursuit to Arvie . . . Pursuit Pursuit to Arvie!"* Of course, all the while a couple of splotches of color are jumping astern and fighting a duel that sends white spray flying like rain at your head.

I was tangled in lines and had one foot in a bucket as first I grabbed one rod and gave the hook a good set and then, for a moment, couldn't make up my mind what to do next. I loosened the drag, put the rod back in the rod holder, and grabbed the other one and set that hook too. Then I grabbed the first rod with what I thought was a free hand—but I had the rods crossed and the second rod's drag was set a wee bit too tight. I straightened it out for a moment, trying to decide on some course of action. By now one of the fish was a couple of hundred yards out and "greyhounding" right past "Pursuit." All I could hear was that captain yelling on the radio, *"Do you need any help?"* Well now, if you were to shut your eyes for a brief moment and join me on the stern of my boat, you would see that I was too helpless even to answer. I just stood there and nodded my head like a horse.

It happened as I, in all the confusion, expected: The largest Sailfish went for a tailwalk and threw out the hook. With only one fish

"I used my thumbs", I told him.

left to handle, the bubblegum and feathers melted away, although I still had a tangle of sorts that could pass for spaghetti.

In about ten minutes more I had the smaller Sailfish up to the boat, I also had ten or fifteen tournament boats standing by. Most looked down at me with obvious envy, but the captain of the magnificent "Pursuit" whispered low: "What did you use?"

"Mostly my thumbs," I whispered back.

Saltwater Fun Fish

Great Barracuda

Here we go, with all of the pleasant devils in the sea. I'm sure you understand that when I say "with all," I don't mean with everything else that swims: only pleasant devils—and that will still leave quite a few "pleasures" unaccounted for.

These fish are the ones you are most likely to encounter when you are out after someone else, or someone else is away on a trip—or perhaps out of season.

Also understand that quite a few of the fish I'll list as fun fish are truly game fish and recognized as such: They are often fish that travel lonely routes and are nowhere common; or they might, perhaps, be pesky fellows who seem designed for little purpose except to test your skill. Some are good to eat, some just so-so, and others not good at all.

Most, but not all, can be taken on artificials, and I'd even qualify that "not" to "rarely." Take the Sheepshead of Eastern southern waters. Most fishermen that you meet will say "impossible" to take on a lure. Well, they are almost right, which means they're wrong. I've caught a number on small micro jigs in pink and blue, but I'll admit I wouldn't make a career of it . . . if there were Fiddler Crabs around.

I'm convinced by now that you and your Dad are pretty good and can take your fish on lures, so I'll simply list the fish and add a sketch so that you will know who is who. I'll even drop a clue or two, as if you didn't know. The best way to handle this funfish routine is for me to list some of the fish that you will meet, and the part of the country where you will shake a hand to a fin, say hello, and have fun.

Fun Fish of the Southeastern States and the Gulf of Mexico

THE BARRACUDA:

Say hello to the GREAT BARRACUDA (*Sphyraena barracuda*), but keep your relationship formal. He has been known to turn and attack. Some people fear him as much as they would "Jaws," which is plain, downright silly. I personally think of him more in the terms of a stray dog, certainly equipped to give you a bite but generally shy. I have found in my dealings with all sorts of dogs (which I love) that a live-and-let-live attitude is all that's expected. I just go about my own business and that is that. I would never provoke any animal or tease it into a bite. Every Barracuda I've ever met (and they number in the thousands) had a similar attitude. For the most part they were all rather curious, and if they were cruising they gave me no qualms at all. On the other hand when I'd see a Barracuda circle a hole in the reef, or obviously stake out a particular bit of the turf, I'd respect it and back off. As I would with a dog who is jealous of his own backyard, I would never invite a Barracuda to push his claim all the way. Like many fish, they are attracted to bright shiny objects, and they have the power to take them away from you. The moral, of course, is don't wear bright shiny things when you go swimming with them and they'll leave you alone. Incidentally, as an old spearfisherman from way back, I urge you not to try to spear one. It's a feat that's not easy. I've never met a Barracuda yet that didn't leave me with the impression that he knew all about spear-guns. Barracudas usually stand well out of range. The real danger is not that they will retaliate for what they suspect you are going to try, but that if you succeed and don't hit them just right they'll come spinning down the shaft of your spear, thrashing about like any bonafide meat chopper would do—and believe me that could be dangerous.

Anyway, enjoy them. They are reasonably safe if you leave them alone, except with a rod, and then they are the best kind of fun. They are easy to tempt with a bucktail, a plug, or a spoon. They'll give you a battle you won't soon forget. They are strong and fairly good jumpers and come in a very good size, up to five feet and a hundred pounds weight; the average would be about twenty pounds (and most of that muscle and teeth).

The Great Barracuda's range is throughout the Caribbean, the Bahamas, and southern Florida. He is found off shore in the Gulf and in the Atlantic in the Gulf Stream up to about North Carolina. But the Florida Keys is where I'd go looking for him, out on the flats, or under the bridges. You are liable to meet him almost any old place in tropical waters. *Use a leader made of wire* (remember his teeth). When you have caught one, let him go. Barracuda are not particularly safe on the table either; the meat can often be toxic and it's not worth the chance. This is particularly true in the West Indies where I suspect they feed on Parrotfish, a colorful Wrasse that eats poison coral among other things.

P.S.: My heart's not into all of this maligning of a truly wonderful fish. In a way these are things I *must* say, just so you'll exercise caution. Frankly, I love the great "cudas" and hope you will too.

This next group of fun fish are not dangerous at all (unless you have a heart condition and can't stand the strain of laughing and yelling all at the same time).

The JACKS:

A large family of fishes (67 or so). The family is called the Carangidae and includes all of the Jacks, Amberjacks, Pompano, Threadfins, Roosterfish, Lookdowns, and Scads.

Because it is such a large group of fighters and because the method of taking them is generally the same from fish to fish, I think it unnecessary to list each of them individually. It is far more important, I should think, that you recognize the fact that you have managed to capture one of the 67 species (a number of which I've drawn for you). As I've mentioned before when we spoke of the Mackerel, the tail is a dead giveaway that you have indeed taken one of the Carangidae. The shape of their tails is *falcate* like this:

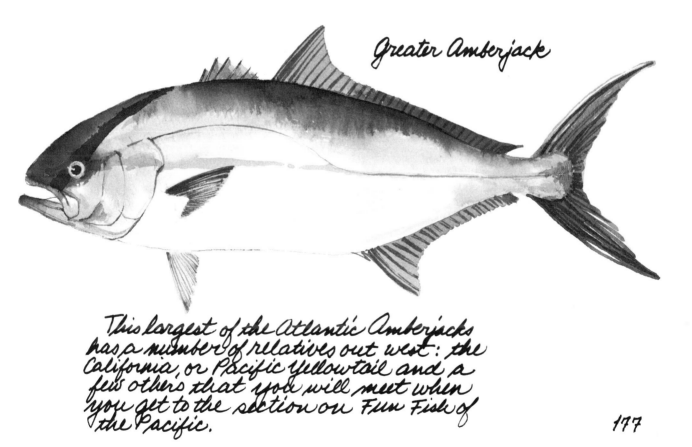

Greater Amberjack

This largest of the Atlantic Amberjacks has a number of relatives out west: the California, or Pacific Yellowtail and a few others that you will meet when you get to the section on Fun Fish of the Pacific.

177

There are three Jacks that you are very likely to encounter in the waters of the southeastern United States. They are the Jack Crevalle, the Blue Runner, and the Bar Jack.

Bar or Skip Jack
We used to call him a "jumpin' jack". He's one of the very few Jacks that do occasionally jump. He has a soft, silvery look, and sometimes a bright blue stripe down his back.

Jack Crevalle
A tough little guy who is easy to love. He's also quite pretty, with pale yellow fins.

Blue Runner (or Blue Crevalle)
We used to call this little blue jack a pest. But only when we were fishing for Pompano.

The CREVALLE is far and away the most common. Any body of saltwater from the Carolinas down to Brazil has a few, if not an army, of them hanging about. There is absolutely no trick at all to hooking a Crevalle (generally referred to as simply the JACK). However landing one is by no means as easy; they hit hard and fight hard. To find out for yourself, just mosey on down to the beach or the bay and plop in a bucktail. Give it a few whips, rather fast, and sooner or later a Jack will come along and try to take it away from you.

Anybody can go out and catch Jacks, but of course you will take more than anyone else, because you have gotten this far in the book (and experts always do better).

Jacks travel in schools (and for them school never lets out). They are found close at hand every month of the year.

Most of the Jacks that you take will be rather small, about two to five pounds; don't let their size deceive you, for, like dynamite, they are powerful stuff in small packages. You will, of course, be fishing them with reasonably light outfits in order to have the most fun, but watch out! If a big one comes along, say about thirty pounds, you'll more than have your hands full (you will probably have time only to say hello and goodby). As with most fish, the really *big ones* are rare. Just know in advance that *IF* you manage to hook one and hold on, you'd better be prepared to give up your plans for the evening. A big Jack will never give up, and you will need plenty of time and luck to bring him to boat or to shore.

By the way, you will recognize a Jack by his fight long before you can see him. Not only do they hit hard and swim fast, but they constantly are shaking their heads, and every shake is a jolt to the rod and right up your arms. I imagine that a Jack that weighed forty pounds would send you enough jolts to keep you on your toes for a year or two afterward.

Now for the best places to look. The dropoff near a main channel in a pass or any place with a good tide running (either in or out), off bridges, and in canals around where there are mangroves and fairly deep water nearby. They love the mouth of a river and any place where you might find oyster beds near channels. You will probably run into them when you are out fishing for Snook or even Bonefish (they kind of like the same places). What you should do is to give a good cast and let your lure sink almost to the bottom. Now retrieve with a modified whip, just a hair slower than you did for the Mackerel. Color seems somewhat unimportant to Jacks; they like yellow and pink and all whites and red-and-white (which is my favorite). Be it known that they will also hit spoons and plugs as well as the bucktails and dudes (try one of your Rapalas, in a magnum size, of course).

I am quite aware that you might well hook somebody else when you are fishing just for the fun of it. Lots of fish hang around in the same waters as Jacks. But tell Dad that the chances are as good as five to one that the first fish you will take will be Mr. Jack.

Almost all of the Jacks are pretty poor eating, so when he grunts (and he will) let him go.

Speaking of eating, put a bib on and meet one of the family that is one of the finest-eating fish in the sea: the POMPANO. There are a number of species of Pompano, but the one that you are most apt to meet is called the COMMON (he is sometimes in some places called the "Sunfish"). His scientific name is *Trachinotus carolinus*. He is a shallow-water species; you might find him almost any place that you

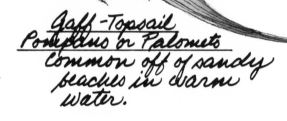

I've drawn for you the _Round Pompano_. When he reaches a large size (up to 50 pounds), he is called the "Permit". The small, common Pompano looks very much like him, only less round.

Gaff-Topsail Pompano or Palometo
Common off of sandy beaches in warm water.

look down
Every time I catch one of these funny little guys I always wonder what he'd look like wearing a pair of sunglasses.

Scad
Just so you'll know what the scads look like. I always think of them as being made of asbestos and wire.

are apt to find Jack. He particularly likes sandbars and the edge of the surf, where he roots around looking for his favorite food, the little sand bugs, or sand fleas as I call them.

The lure that most Pompano fishermen rely on is a small yellow nylon dude, worked with a rhythm that will soon have you dancing along. It goes like this: cast and let your jig sink to the bottom. Now bring up the tip of your rod rather smartly and let the lure sink back down (take a couple of cranks on your reel handle as it sinks). Now bring it up again with a double bump-bump; let it sink, crank, and give a bump. Cast, sink, bump, crank, sink, bump-bump (pause), and repeat bumping and cranking and letting it sink. The action is in reality a *very slow "whip."* Think of the sand bug hopping along on the bottom. Try to visualize it, and make your lure behave like you think a small, jumping, bug-like Crab might behave.

When you or your Dad can stand next to a grizzled and leathery old bridge fisherman who keeps talking about "pomps" and you outfish him, consider yourself the best in the world.

This is one fish that I seldom let go, unless he's a runt. Pompano, besides being so wonderful to eat, are not that easy to come by. In the waters where I fished as a kid (pretty good Pompano water at that), we considered two fish a day a mighty fine catch, so don't go out expecting to come home in an hour loaded down with a bag full of Pomps. Another common Pompano in Florida is the ROUND POM-PANO (*Trachinotus falcatus*). He grows to a very large size (for Pompano), at least 50 pounds. When he grows up, he is called a Permit. He is the one that I drew a picture of. He's a whiz and a bang on a flyrod (if you are skillful and lucky).

Next say hello to the LADYFISH (possibly goodby). This is a hard fish to hold, as this little lady (*Esops saurus*) believes in living it up in the air.

She is much like a small Tarpon both in looks and in action (also not unlike the Bonefish at first glance).

I think that any fisherman who has ever caught this game little fish falls in love—and why not? She is a petite ballerina who lives in the sea; if she has any faults it's the rough company she hangs out with, all those free-for-all fighters, the Jacks and the Snook, for she is frequently caught when you are out after much rougher game. But

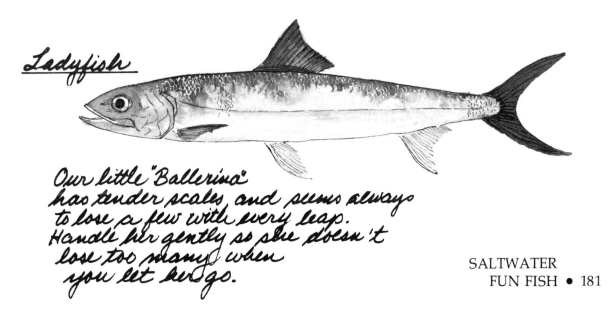

Ladyfish

Our little "Ballerina" has tender scales, and seems always to lose a few with every leap. Handle her gently so she doesn't lose too many when you let her go.

then, just you be happy, for the contrast is delightful as she grace-
fully takes to the air in leap after leap. By the way, the Ladyfish is in
some places referred to as the TEN POUNDER (but don't be misled).
Although she *might* occasionally reach such a weight, it would be an
exception. She averages about three to five pounds. A secret you
might let Dad in on is: Remember when we were talking about
"figure-eighting" for Snook off the bridge with a lantern at night.
Well, one of those shadows most certainly will be a Ladyfish. So
carry a spinning rod and some Rapalas and/or jigs. This would be
the best time of all to catch a truly "ten pounder."

By the way, I've seen some pretty mean and stupid acts in my
time. One of them, and a pet peeve, is the "fisherman" who catches
Ladyfish by the tens off of the bridges at night and just leaves them
to die. They are very poor eating and you must let them go. After
all, as a ballerina she danced you her version of the beautiful and
tragic *Swan Lake.* Applaud and give her a good round of bravos, but
don't make the ending for real.

Meet a couple of SNAPPERS:

The most common of them throughout Florida and points south is
the GRAY or MANGROVE SNAPPER (*Lutjanus griseus*). He is perhaps the
greatest challenge that you can present to your Dad. He is shyer
than the freshwater Trouts and a good deal smarter than almost
anyone else you might meet. When you are out wading or moving a
skiff through the shallow clear water near mangroves, you will
undoubtedly see him. Watch how he watches you, and I'll bet you
can tell what he thinks. Don't be embarrassed because he thinks you
are dumb. After all, what does a fish know for sure?

mangrove or Gray
snapper
The dark slash over
his eye makes
him look like a
bandit. (and he
is!)

If you want to catch him, you'll have to try every trick in the book.
(The chances are that he's already at work dictating a new and more
advanced copy.) Sneak around and go *light,* the smallest of lines and
the lightest of lures. He will take little bucktails and small plugs and
spoons, but not if he sees you. The best chance you might have is
out on the flats if the water's a little bit cloudy and you are fishing a
fairly deep hole. If everything else fails, tell Dad that you'll forgive
him just this once if in a fit of frustration he resorts to a small hook
and live Shrimp. All of the Snappers are wonderful eating, so any

extra effort you might make is probably worth it. And besides, if you take one on lure, he's something special to brag about.

Other Snappers you are liable to take are:

The DOG SNAPPER (*Lutjanus jocu*). He gets his name from his teeth, which are more prominent than those of his cousins. His look very much like a dog's fangs.

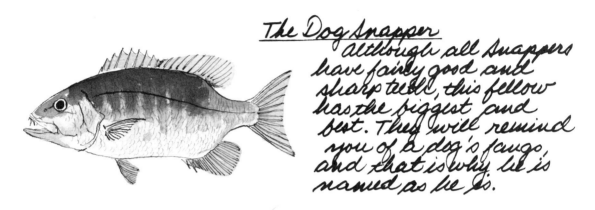

The Dog Snapper
although all Snappers have fairly good and sharp teeth, this fellow has the biggest and best. They will remind you of a dog's fangs, and that is why he is named as he is.

The MUTTON SNAPPER (*Lutjanus analis*) comes in a pretty good package and size. He reaches a weight of about twenty-some pounds, although the average is somewhere between five and ten. He likes slightly deeper water than the Gray. Look for him around coral reefs and the deeper holes. You might also keep your eyes open when you are out fishing the flats; once in a while he'll appear in the clear shallow water. I've caught a number while fishing for Bonefish.

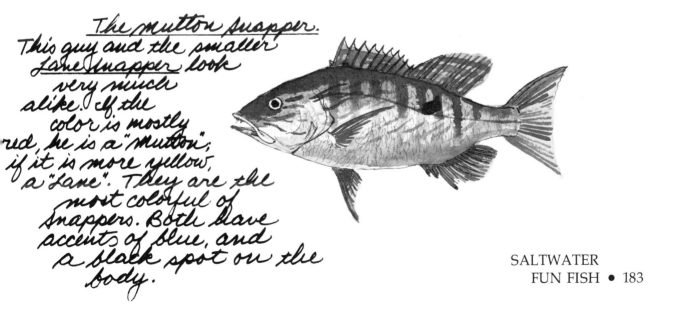

The mutton snapper.
This guy and the smaller Lane Snapper look very much alike. If the color is mostly red, he is a "mutton"; if it is more yellow, a "Lane". They are the most colorful of snappers. Both have accents of blue, and a black spot on the body.

The LANE SNAPPER (*Lutjanus synagris*) is colored and marked very much like the Mutton Snapper. He tends more to the yellow, while the Mutton Snapper has a good deal more red. The Lane however is a very small fish, usually a pound or less. He only occasionally will take a lure, but when he does you're in for a fine eating treat.

One word of caution: All of the Snappers have good, sharp teeth. Use a very fine wire leader, just in case.

The REDFISH or CHANNEL Bass or RED DRUM (*Sciaenops ocellata*) is known by any one of the three names. I prefer Redfish, probably because I'm from Florida. If you were to take him up in Virginia or the Carolinas, you'd more often hear Channel Bass. At any rate, his color is a somewhat reddish bronze (in certain lights he really looks red). You can spot him by his spot, or in some cases spots, near his tail. He loves shallow bays and oyster-bed country. You'll also see him cruising along either alone or sometimes in schools out over the grass flats, probably looking for Crabs (his favorite food), though he also likes Mullet and other smaller fish. So it's not much of a trick to catch him on lures. Just work your bucktail or plug rather slow and close to the bottom. Redfish reach a pretty fair size; the largest ever caught weighed 83 pounds. Most, however, run from ten to twenty pounds, with an occasional forty-pounder bonus.

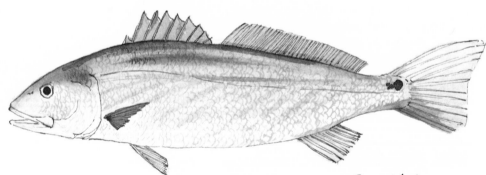

Redfish
also called Red Drum and Channel Bass
This is the guy who always gave me such a rough time when I was little and fished with fiddlers.

I've thrown in a family of "big mouths" for your pleasure: the Groupers. They are always around and ready to take your lure and head for a hole in the rocks.

They belong to the family Serranidae, which is a very large family indeed, perhaps as large as the Smiths and the Joneses. There are more than 400 species all over the world. At least 50 members are found in Florida waters alone. Of course we can't possibly introduce them all to your Dad, but a picture of one or two tells the whole story. They all look remarkably alike from head to tail. Coloration and pattern does vary greatly, from small red spots on the Red Hind, to blotches and or marbling and bars in many shades of red, brown, black, yellow, grey, and even touches of white as found on the Snowy Grouper. They run a wide range of size, from a couple of pounds, like most of the Hinds, to the gigantic Jewfish, who can reach a weight in excess of 700 pounds. I would say that the average size of the family is somewhat less than 50 pounds, perhaps closer to 20.

We shall discuss only three of the family, the ones you and your Dad are most likely to "luck" into.

The NASSAU GROUPER (*Epinephelus striatus*) is rather common in Florida waters and is found where you have rocky bottoms and reefs, as well as around pilings and wrecks, anything in fact that he can run and hide in (all Groupers appear to value the same type of sea terrain). The only difference is in their individual preferences as to depth of the water. The *deep* dwellers are of little interest to us who fish for sport. Fortunately for us, most species like medium depth to shallow water throughout the tropics.

dark sploch

nassau grouper

The Red Grouper has markings very similar to the "Nassau". He is lighter in tone and quite red. He never has the dark mark on the top of the base of his tail.

Another popular guy is the RED GROUPER (*Epinephelus morio*). Look for him in the same places as Mr. Nassau. Identify him, of course, by his overall reddish color.

The BLACK GROUPER (*Mycteroperca bonaci*) might dart out and grab at your lure when you are expecting one of the others. He will have dark squarish blotches and irregular lines that are pale grey. Like all of the Groupers, he will take artificials, plugs and spoons, feathers, and various jigs. You will need a medium-light to medium outfit for Groupers, as you are very likely apt to tie into a fish of some size

SALTWATER
FUN FISH • 185

and you must try your best to stop him before he can get back to his hole in the reef. If he makes it, you are the one who might as well throw in the sponge.

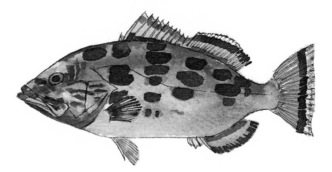

Black Grouper
This Grouper is the best fighter of the well known "Florida Groper Gang".

The COBIA or CRAB EATER (*Rachycentron canadum*) we'll just mention in passing. (I did, however, take the time to draw the portrait of this wonderful fish for you.) Just in case you and your Dad might spot one or two cruising by on the beach or under the bridge, you'll know who he is. Cobias are fairly large, brown-colored fish that I always for some reason take to be a Shark when I first spot one. I suppose because they are not everywhere common (they are more so in the Gulf of Mexico). There is some specialized fishing for these guys out around the oil rigs offshore in the Gulf. You might give it a try if ever the chance comes along. They are very strong fighters and will occasionally leap. They average about thirty pounds and are delicious eating. They will take your bucktails and plugs. I hope that you and your Dad don't get too excited and confuse them with Sharks (like I do) when one comes along. Just whip out a lure and hope for the best.

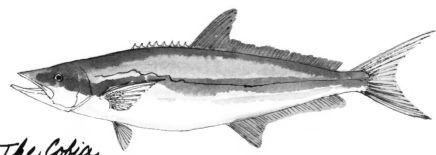

The Cobia
also called Crabeater and Ling
I've also heard him referred to as "Lemon Ling", and why, I don't know. As you can see, he doesn't look at all like a lemon (doesn't taste or fight like one either).

An offshore fish that I list as a fun fish (although he rightfully belongs up there with the ''great'' ones) is the WAHOO (*Acanthocybium solandri*). Mostly he just happens. Rarely do you go out just to fish him (I suppose some very smart people do). Usually he's picked up when you are far out to sea looking for Tuna or Sailfish and Marlin. As far as I know, Wahoo never travel in schools. Lonely fellows, they just pop up when you least expect them. But what a fight they can give: as fast as any fish in the sea, they dazzle with speed, first running here and then a sudden change in direction, perhaps straight at and under the boat. You seldom have time to react until he's straightened you out in the new direction he's decided to travel. The average Wahoo will be about or close to 100 pounds. I hope you have fun. Look for his picture and a story when you get to the section on fun fish of the West Coast and think of his cousin, the King Mackerel.

To see what he looks like, turn to page 200 for a picture of the "Wahoo".

I've saved the SPOTTED SEATROUT (*Cynoscion nebulosus*) for the last. If you haven't guessed why, I will tell you. It's not because he's the best, but because I love him the most. He is the magic of my boyhood years, a fish to depend on. He is beautiful and always eager to do battle, and besides I once caught one that's far bigger than any ever recorded! 17 pounds 9 ounces. Caught him on a Finger Mullet that I had netted. Caught him off the beach of Sarasota Pass in front of my house in 1938. At first I thought I had hooked a Tarpon when he rolled silver and bright twenty yards out. Everybody agreed that he was far and away the largest Trout they'd ever seen. We oh-hed and ah-hed and then ate him, as any sensible Florida family would do. I was as proud as any boy could ever have been, and I guess it wasn't until a few years later I learned about records and immortality. As you know, I never did care. If I were to catch him today, I'd give a great sigh of love and let him go on his way. And even if I were the only one to know his great size, I would treasure the moment he gave me more than a shoulder patch or a plaque or ten sterling cups.

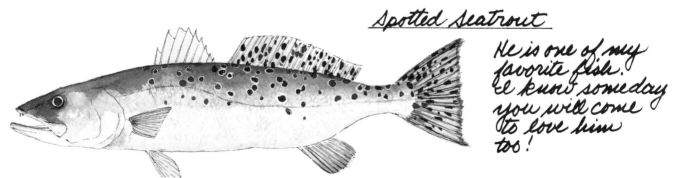

Spotted Seatrout

He is one of my favorite fish. I know someday you will come to love him too!

My favorite bucktails for Seatrout are ½ oz. in yellow and white or white and red (I make my own from a cast of my own design, but look for an Upperman lure if they are still around), and you can't go wrong with a Rapala in silver, floating 13G-magnum size. Mirror lures are also top producers.

Further up the Coast in the East:

Unlike the Deep South, I'm not particularly enthused by the saltwater fun fish possibilities up north. But on the other hand, the fishing is so first-rate for the big Bluefish and Stripers and Tunas I don't really care that the variety is not that all great. (You should have action enough the whole summer through.) But as is the rule, there are always a couple of species of fish waiting to fill in the gaps when you need them. Of course, please realize that I refer to fish that can be taken with artificials. For sure there are fish in the north that the baitfishermen can enjoy on the side, like the Tautog or Blackfish and the delicious but small Winter Flounders.

Now Flounder suggests at least one fish that readily takes lures, and that is the FLUKE or SUMMER FLOUNDER (*Paralichthys dentatus*). He's a guy who likes sandy bottoms in the bays and the sound and is also found over the sand bars close in to shore at the ocean. I would suggest that you try trolling him up, using a good flashy spoon, spinner, and/or bucktail in white or red and white. Keep your troll fairly steady and slow; give your bucktail a good hopping action. Sometimes a bit of pork rind attached helps bring them in.

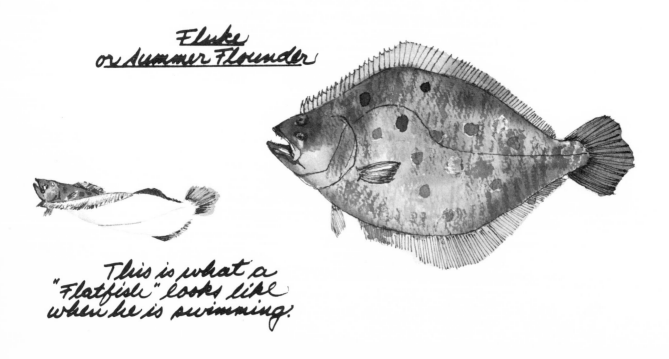

Fluke or Summer Flounder

This is what a "Flatfish" looks like when he is swimming.

The WEAKFISH (*Cynoscion regalis*): As you may well remember, this is the guy that was responsible for my catching my first Striped Bass. He is also a cousin to the Spotted Seatrout of my Florida days. So it certainly follows that I have a special place in my heart for this fish.

Weakfish

He has quite a history, and indeed it's quite an unhappy one. It is a story of waste. I have heard stories and read books and articles that dealt with this sad aspect of fishing. Long ago, sometime around the turn of the century, the Weakfish was so numerous up in the Peconic Bay area that there was nothing at all to loading a skiff to the gunwales with "weaks" any morning of the summer. The "fishermen" came by the thousands and enjoyed their sport, taking tens of thousands of these magnificent game little fish. Then after the pictures and congratulations all around, the fish were piled high and left along the road back to the city. There they rotted, week after week; they say that the stench covered the land on the "better" weekends. Many of the fish, yellow-finned "tide runners," were ten and twelve pounds, weights that would be unbelievable today when any weight even close to five pounds is cause to rejoice. The fish have never recovered.

Pollution, of course, plays a role in the tragedy, as well as the increased pressure from both the sportfishing and the commercial interests. You will still, however, enjoy some light tackle sport in quiet small harbors and bays from Virginia north: the Chesapeake and Delaware bays, Long Island Sound, and into the Peconic Bay system. Look for Weakfish in tide rips and rather shallow water, in sloughs and up saltwater creeks that run through the marshes. Because of limited numbers today, the best way to take a few fish for the table is, of course, by chumming and fishing with bait; Shrimp are considered the best. You might also try Blood Worms and Sand Worms or Crabs. If you decide to stick to your lures (and I hope that you will) try small bucktails and spoons. The idea is to be out on the extreme shallow bays at daybreak (when it is pretty). If you are lucky, you will spot schools of fish foraging at the surface. Cast ahead of them a few feet and give your *bucktail* the bottom-bouncing and -hopping action of Shrimp. The strike when it comes is decisive and strong. The first run a Weakfish makes will lead you to believe that you are into a much larger fish. They are excellent eating, so take a couple home. Don't leave them by the side of the road.

The SCUP or, more commonly, just PORGY (*Stenotomus chrysops*):

Most people think I am daft when I say "I only go after him with lures." "They" will argue and insist that he can be taken only on bait. Well, I let "them" think what they will, and then I go out and have a great deal of fun; not to mention the fact that they don't believe the size of the Porgies I bring home. Most of these rather small fish that I catch average two to three and four pounds. I once caught one up off Block Island that went just a shade under five pounds.

I use ¼ oz. white-and-red bucktails exclusively. I fish in the surf on New England beaches or on the islands offshore like at Martha's Vineyard or Block Island. It's a wonderful way to while away time as you sunbathe and wait for the evening and a crack at the Stripers. Fish your bucktail in about the same manner that you did when you went fishing for Pompano, down near the bottom, with the "bump-rest-bump-bump" rhythm; it can be faster rather than slow. Be prepared as a big Porgy hits with a "thump-thump," *no rest,* and a "thump."

Scup or Porgy

Another guy that you might try your hand at come the "dog days" of summer is the BLACK SEA BASS (*Centropristis striata*). He is a sporty small fish that will run from two to five pounds. Most are taken on bait fished near the bottom; but take heart, as he also enjoys striking an artificial. The diamond jig with chrome finish is possibly the best type; as second choice I would prefer the old standby, the *bucktail,* in pale yellow or white. The Sea Bass seems to prefer clear and fairly deep water, twenty to one hundred feet; he loves wrecks and/or hard rocky bottoms. Sometimes in the earlier spring you might find a few of the smaller Bass scattered throughout the bay. Look for shellfish beds in ten to fifteen feet of water. These fish also lurk around docks and pilings or jetties where the current is reasonably fast. They are an important and delicious food fish so are

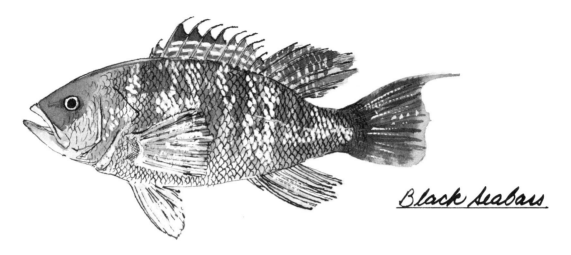

Black Seabass

well worth your time and effort. Use medium-light spinning outfits for the most fun.

The top of the line of the fun fish up north (if you just want a fight to remember) is the BONITO (*Sarda sarda*). He is a little Tuna-type fish (some fishermen refer to them as "Tuna wearing pajamas"; that's because of their stripes). They come close inshore, right off the mouths of the inlets. If you are lucky and spot a big school feeding on top, rush right on up, kill the motor, and drift. You can cast almost any type of lure and be assured of a smashing strike as soon as it touches the water. They are great fun on a saltwater flyrod, using any of the flashy type streamers. Although most of the Bonitos you'll meet will be rather small, three to seven pounds, don't feel superior on account of *your* size; you'd have to be a five-hundred-pound weightlifter to be on the safe side.

Ask Dad if he thinks that all seas and oceans are different one from the other. Be a bit more specific and ask, "Do some of the same fish that live in Florida also live in the waters of the Pacific near California?" His answer might go all over the lot and surprise you. He might say yes, and he'd be partially right, or he might say no and get part of the other part right, or he might say yes and no, surprising you with the depth of his knowledge.

Now is the time to straighten it all out for him.

The Atlantic Bonito

SALTWATER
FUN FISH • 191

Tell him he will feel right at home from Southern California through Baja California (of course—and beyond).

He will meet quite a few of his old Florida friends and a few so closely related that even scientists haven't been able to straighten them out. He'll also meet some members of families he knew. Of course they are cousins and sport different spots and/or stripes. Some may grow larger than their Florida kin, and some slightly smaller. Naturally Dad's no takes care of itself, for surely you'll find an occasional oddball who doesn't have family or friends anyplace else.

Now because most of the fish on the West Coast are so similar in their habits and needs to the fun fish you've already met, I'll just list them and throw in a few clues like best times of the year and/or best places to go if you are to catch them.

Fun Fish on the West Coast:

Not enough people practice the art of fishing with lures in the saltwater out west. They have been conditioned to live-bait fishing, using Sardines and Anchovies since the days of the Gold Rush (almost). But you and I know at this point that somebody is missing a great deal of fun.

I remember the old argument: "Who has the best oranges?" Well, naturally I defended my wonderful state of Florida and her oranges, and I'm certainly not going to start a new war about fish. Besides, everyone knows that *lemons* go better with fish and that, indeed, California has outstanding lemons and wonderful fish.

As we know from our study of fish in the East, the variety of species multiplied by leaps and bounds the further south we traveled, and so it is with the fishing out West.

From the State of Washington down through Oregon and Northern California, the big deals are the Pacific Salmon and, of course, the Striped Bass from around San Francisco and its bay. Most Salmon are taken by trolling rigged, natural baits, Herring, Anchovies, or Pacific Sardines. They will also hit plugs and spoons. But lures are nowhere as productive as the naturals. So I suggest that when in those parts you bend to the local tradition and drag a Herring around. No matter, you will always be proud of taking one of these wonderful bright silver fish any way that you can.

Conditions start to improve for the lure fisherman as he moves in range of the Stripers in Northern California. I would have you suggest to your Dad that he fish them as he has learned to do in the East. Now things really start moving as we progress down the coast toward the southern border. As the water warms up, so does the fishing. It almost seems that for every few miles that we make headed south, we are able to add new fun to our list, so please be prepared for an explosion of fish when we reach the Baja Peninsula and the Sea of Cortez down in Old Mexico—*olé!*

Here is a list of just a *few* of the fish that you and your Dad might happen to meet on a visit to Southern California and south of the border down Mexico way.

Albacore (Thunnus alalunga):

We mentioned this long-finned *Tuna* in the chapter on these strong wonderful fish. Well, as I said, the Pacific is the place to go and catch them. They are one of the big attractions off Southern California. They appear about the first of July and hang around until late September or into October. Albacore are one Tuna that only rarely come in close to shore. You have to travel to get them, usually from fifty to one hundred miles off the beach. It is well worth the trip. Again, Californians seem to prefer the live-bait fishing technique, so go ahead and have fun. Just remember that the Albacore loves lures also. It wouldn't be at all out of line if you were to carry a few of your favorite *bucktails* along.

Pacific Barracuda (Sphyraena argentea):

This little guy (sigh of relief) is not dangerous at all, and even a big one about ten or twelve pounds (which is about as big as they grow) would only be a mouthful for the Great Barracuda of Florida. He is found close into shore as well as out by all of the offshore islands. The time of the year to hope for him off California is spring through summer. He absolutely dotes on little white bucktails and smaller Rapalas. Here is a chance to try out your Florida whip in the Pacific. Like all Barracudas, they fall for a fast retrieve.

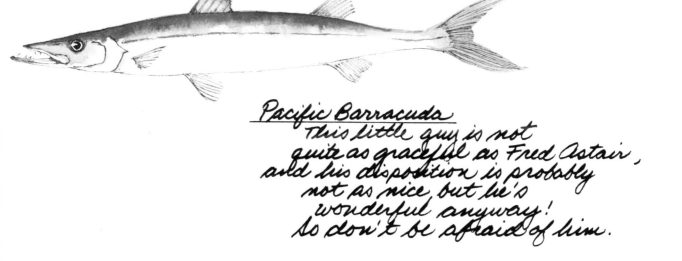

Pacific Barracuda
This little guy is not quite as graceful as Fred Astair, and his disposition is probably not as nice but he's wonderful anyway! So don't be afraid of him.

Bonito, Skipjack, and Little Tunas:

There are a number of these wild little Tunalike fish that range up and down the Coast. In the more northernly part of their range off San Francisco—even up further—summertime fishing is best. These are warm-water lovers and therefore, of course, are more numerous the further south you go. In Mexican waters they provide steady sport most of the year. They travel in very large schools, and always seem to be willing to take on anything that you are willing to try in the way of lures. Feathers and bucktails I think they really like best; try them in white, yellow, blue, and/or green (perhaps even black).

BONITO particularly come close into shore, and at times are taken right in the harbors and off the many fishing piers. They are a fine hefty fish to take on a saltwater flyrod; try any bright and attractive streamer. I think it quite safe to say that any of these guys might well become one of Dad's favorite fun fish if he uses fairly light tackle. I have one special spinning outfit that I carry just for these fish. It's a 5½ foot fiberglass rod with a fast action tip, a Daiwa 1500 C reel, and 8 pound test line; actually it's a versatile little saltwater outfit for any number of bright fast little fish. But good heavens! Don't try it on Marlin.

Corvina:

Here is a family of old friends. At least they belong to the same gang as the Weakfish and Spotted Seatrout of the East, the great family *Cynoscion*. The West undoubtedly has the edge in both the number of species and the range in their sizes. Let's list a few that you are apt to meet. Don't fall out of your chair when you hear how big a couple of them grow.

The Gulf Corvina (Cynoscion othonopterus):

is sometimes and in certain places called the SCALYFIN CORVINA. He might weigh as high as 6 to 8 pounds. He can be taken right off the beach in the surf or in the lagoons over sandy bottom or grass. He likes small plugs and bucktails or spoons. He is far more common in the southern part of his range, which is Baja. He seldom strays north of the border.

The Striped Corvina (Cynoscion reticulatus):

is a Mexican national. He even looks, in a way, as if he's wearing a beautiful striped serape. He grows to about three feet in length, 10 to 12 pounds. Look for him in the back bays of Baja's west coast. The same type of lures are in order as those for the guy above.

The Orange-Mouth Corvina (Cynoscion xanthulus):

is sometimes called the YELLOW-FINNED CORVINA. This is the guy who was introduced to the Salton Sea (an inland body of saltwater in Southern California). He grows to a size of some 30 pounds (see how much bigger we are getting). His principal range is in the Sea of

Many of the Corvinas look a great deal alike. Their names usually suggest what to look for to tell them apart.

Cortez from its top down to its middle. He takes a wide variety of lures and is a sucker for bright wobbling spoons. Try the new spoon put out by Mepps in gold # 3.

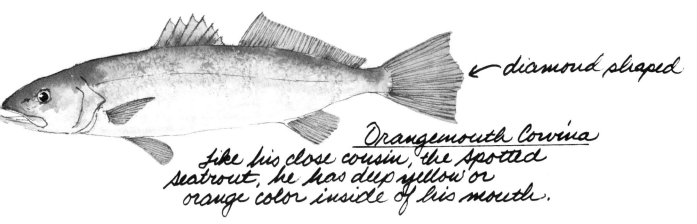

← *diamond shaped*

Orangemouth Corvina

like his close cousin, the spotted seatrout, he has deep yellow or orange color inside of his mouth.

Shortfin Corvina (Cynoscion parvipinnis):
is a smaller Corvina; he usually weighs in at a couple of pounds. His range is the same as Mr. Orange-Mouth. Just use smaller lures. He's also been introduced into the Salton Sea.

The White Sea Bass (Cynoscion nobilis):
First of all, before he gets all mixed up, tell your Dad that this fish is a Corvina and, despite his name, is not a Sea Bass (anywhich way). Now California gets lucky, for this is one Corvina that travels up north of the border, at least as far as San Francisco. But, of course, he's not at all common up that way. This is one of the big guys known to reach a weight of perhaps 80 pounds, though half of that would be far more common. As a matter of fact, perhaps even half of that would be average, 20 pounds. He loves deep-growing

most Corvinas have rather square tails. As you can see, the Orange-mouth and the Totuava (next page) do not.

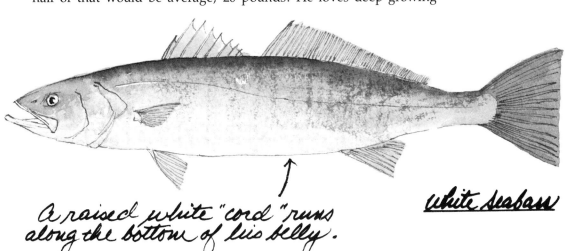

↑
A raised white "cord" runs along the bottom of his belly.

white seabass

kelp beds (kelp is *long* rubbery seaweed). He goes for all sorts of lures: plugs, spoons and feathers, or the bucktail. Fish him deep, close to the bottom. Troll or work your lure *very slowly;* that's the way he likes it.

NOW FOR THE GIANT!

The Totuava (Cynoscion macdonaldi):

How about 300 pounds? How about that? This wonderful gamefish is found only in the upper half of the Sea of Cortez. In January and February he moves to the head of the Gulf for spawning. Remember the story I told you about the Weakfish and waste.

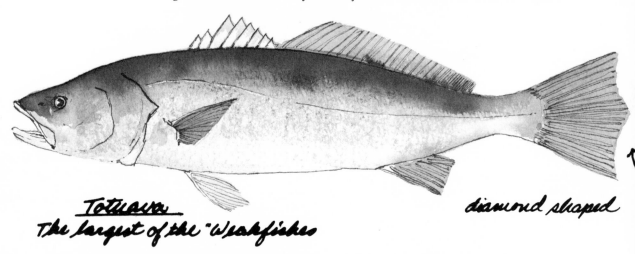

Totuava
The largest of the "Weakfishes

diamond shaped

Well, the same thing happened to this mighty cousin of his, the Totuava. His air bladder was much in demand for a soup, and this great fish was taken just for that purpose. His carcass was left on the beaches to rot. This all happened in the first twenty years of our century, and the Totuava was well on his way to extinction before thinking men put a stop to it. Today he is still under protection at certain times and places, thank goodness. Today there are plenty around in the 150 to 200 pound class. They seem to prefer spoons trolled rather deep, down by the mud on the bottom. Personally if it were up to me, I'd let this fish go. I'm not all that fond of Totuava air bladder soup.

Just to let you know that they are here:

Dolphin:

The fun fish from the Atlantic. He's all over the place down off of Baja. The same rules I've mentioned before apply.

Groupers and Certain Sea Basses (the Family Serranidae):

This large "grouping" of Groupers has the same habits and preferences for lures as those we discussed who live in Florida. They range in size from just a couple of pounds to the giant Southern Jewfish which might reach 1,000 pounds. One other biggie would be the California Giant Black Sea Bass: he reaches a weight of near 600 pounds. If you are amazing and manage to land one of each of these giants on the same trip, you can tell them apart by the shape of the tails which are like this:

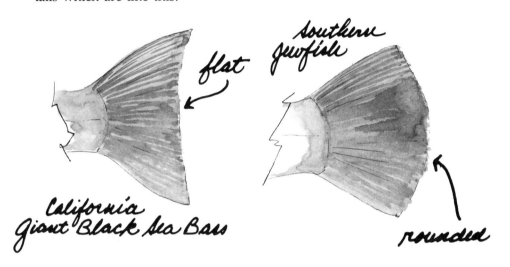

flat

Southern Jewfish

California Giant Black Sea Bass

rounded

Because there are at least thirty-some species of Groupers in the Pacific waters of Southern California and Baja, and it would take a fish biologist to sort them all out (in Florida there were fifty members of the family), I will simply suggest that you look at the pictures of the Florida Groupers. They are typical fish. Then go out and catch whichever comes along. They all like the rocks, holes to hide in, and fairly deep water. They are all good to eat and sporty to catch.

In Mexican waters most of the Basses are called Cabrilla this or Cabrilla that, depending on who is calling. The one guy you are most likely to meet is the CABRILLA PINTO (*Mycteroperca rosacea*). He travels in schools close to the surface (which behavior is different from the way most of his family acts). You will often, down in Baja, meet him near schools of Yellowtail. He will take anything that even looks like a lure, and he will try to beat the much faster Yellowtail to it. He is a fine fighting fish delicious to eat, and once in a while he comes with a surprise: a bright golden color phase that makes him as beautiful as any fish in the sea (this I always let go).

Now a happy reunion. *Elops saurus,* our little ballerina the LADYFISH (actually some scientists call her *Elops affinis* out here in the West where she seems quite at home). Again, down in Baja look for her in shallow water bays and lagoons. Don't expect her to be as plentiful as she was in Florida, for she is not. Just be thankful she's there to give you a dance.

Pacific Jack Mackerel (Trachurus symmetricus):
is a rather small fish, generally less than five pounds. I mention him only because he's such a dependable guy for light-tackle trollers off the California coast. He is found from close inshore to many hundreds of miles out to sea. He particularly likes bright silver spoons.

Pacific Jack Mackerel

not a Mackerel at all, but a scap. which makes him a member in good standing of the jack family.

Pompano:
There are three species (very similar to the Florida kinds): the Pacific Permit, sometimes called the Pancake Pompano (*Trachinotus kennedyi*), the Gafftopsail Pompano (*Trachinotus rhodopus*), and the Paloma Pompano (*Trachinotus paitensis*). There is one other fish called a "Pompano" in Mexican waters, but he's really a Jack. This is the THREADFIN, or more correctly, the THREADFIN JACK (*Citula otrynter*).

Pacific Threadfin Jack

This powerful jack has a cousin back in Florida that we call the African Pompano (who's not a Pompano at all— he, too is a jack!)

The Roosterfish (Nematistius pectoralis):

is a guy that I've chosen for an object lesson for you to give to your Dad. First explain that, as he (Dad) moves to new oceans and seas, he will most likely encounter an oddball or two, fish that are unique (at least in appearance), fish that are quite different from the old friends across country in the ocean back home. The Roosterfish is one. He is found *only* in the eastern Pacific, on the West Coast of the Americas from Baja down to Peru. (Take my word for it.) *Now* study the picture of this strange-looking fish, with his greatly elongated first dorsal fin. Ask Dad, "How would I catch one?" or "What are his habits?" "Does he live very deep?" "Does he travel in schools?"—all sorts of questions like that.

Roosterfish

This "one-of-a-kind" fish is found only in the eastern Pacific, on the west coast of the Americas. Not a great deal is known about his life history. Although I don't know it for sure, I suspect that they spawn and begin life in the northern part of their range — close to the mid-section of the Gulf of California, in the deep water around islands. I once saw a number of small ones, about 6-8", swimming near and around the jellyfish in that area. Although he belongs to his own family (nematistiidae), he is closely related to the jacks.

Of course by now your Dad should be thinking like a true fisherman. He should be solving a few mysteries all on his own. When he can do that, as you know, he will be able to go any place in the world and catch fish. He may not know the name of some particular stranger, but isn't it more important and rewarding to know a great deal about him, like perhaps who some of his relatives are, or where he might swim or what he might eat, the lures he would take and even perhaps what kind of fight to expect? Will he jump or make long dashing runs, or run for the bottom and look for a cave?

Well now, just look at that Roosterfish once again. Perhaps it might help if you partially covered that long dorsal fin with your hand (to make it look a little more like most fish that you'll meet). Study the body and head and pay particular attention to the tail (and all other fins). As you know, the tail shape is one of the strongest of clues.

Does he remind you of anyone else that you've met in the book? Well, take a good look at the Great Amberjack. As a matter of fact, look at any old Jack. Right away you should see that there is a strong relationship between the Rooster and the Jack. As all Jacks generally like the same things, the same kind of foods, the same types of waters, you should have no trouble at all guiding Dad to a fine Roosterfish (as long as you do your guiding down in Baja).

The Wahoo

is the same fast and wonderful fish we met in the East. He is very abundant off the southern end of Baja.

At this point in your lessons for Dad about fish, I think it advisable to add a caution of sorts. It is not, and I'd like to repeat IS NOT, a caution that deals with probable danger at sea. It is not an advisory about fish that might pull off your toe (if you're not very smart).

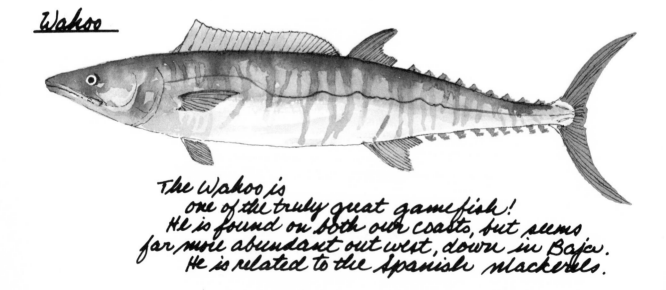

Wahoo

The Wahoo is one of the truly great gamefish! He is found on both our coasts, but seems far more abundant out west, down in Baja. He is related to the Spanish mackerels.

Rather, indeed, it's about the *fisherman's story disease*. You will find, as I've found, that it's an automatic reflex disease of the mind and the tongue. Mention the name of certain great fish and out pops a story. Such a contagious condition is quite under control when you are in the polite and gentle company of other fishermen. In fact, I think you could say that the condition is not only controlled, but the contagion is usually and deliberately spread. But *WATCH OUT* for your *nonfishing friends*, unless you enjoy watching their eyes glaze over like the carrots on the side of your plate of broiled Pompano. I never, but never, expect to dine out at a restaurant that features seafood with my nonfishing friends. You have no idea, but they do, as to just what one of those menus can do when I'm there. So a cheer for dining out with nonfishing friends on spaghetti—or perhaps enchiladas.

HOORAY and WAHOO!

Which remind me to tell you a story.

Wahoo are to my mind the fastest fish in the sea. I've caught only two, and each left me stunned for a week. The first one came as quite a surprise (and is the one that the story's about). I was out trolling for Blackfin Tuna, alone except for my old fishing dog Skipper. Now, Skipper loved trolling for Tunas almost more than I did. He would sit up on the bridge acting as spotter, and I can tell you he was a mighty fine Tuna spotter at that. He would sit with his ears standing erect and his eyes filled with a constant excitement. He could spot a school of Tuna at well over a mile. Then he would start to bark hysterically and carry on like a fool as only a good Tuna-spotting dog knows how to do.

Here's how he and I worked as a team: on his alert (which sounded as though World War Three had just arrived at my starboard horizon), I would head in the direction he indicated, knowing that on the very first hookup with Tuna, Skipper would be down off the bridge in a flash to lend me a paw, which bless his sweet willing soul always created a tangle and hardship. (I have always been careful not to let him know that I really felt this way.)

Well, as expected on such a fine Tuna day, Skipper started to bark. I looked to the point of his interest and saw nothing at all. Then he started to whine, then his head jerked around as if he might have been a mixture of Belgian Shepherd and owl. I was alarmed that he might have broken his neck (for that's how violently his head snapped around), and I was even more sure of it when he started having a fit. At that precise moment, the fish hit. The strike and the run were definitely uncharacteristic of Tuna. I had no idea in the world about who or what I had hooked. For one fleeting moment the thought crossed my mind—submarine—headed for Cuba down west—but suddenly it turned and Bermuda seemed a more likely target. (So it certainly wasn't one of our own.)

The fight, I suppose, spun on for a good half hour or more, and in truth is hard to describe, simply because only another Wahoo could possibly understand the wild change of directions; first straight away and here, or zip! he would go a football field's length away over there. Skipper, I think, was far more confused than I was. He never seemed to be able to follow the action, his head snapping back and forth, always in the wrong direction. He even stopped barking after a while, which is a most unusual thing for a Tuna-spotting dog to do or not to do as the case might apply.

Part of the end of the story is, as you probably already know, that I brought the beautiful Wahoo up to the boat and overrode the objections of Skipper and turned the fish loose. But there are a couple of other parts to the ending that I couldn't expect you to know. For one thing, Skipper gave up spotting Tuna and spent the best of many good years out on the sea, snapping his poor head back and forth looking for Wahoo. And last but not least of the ending is a bit of advice that goes with the caution about the "fishermen's story" disease and that is: *IF* you *DO* happen to find yourself dining on seafood with nonfishing friends, *ADD* a dog-fishing-friend to your story and their eyes will never glaze over at all.

When you tell stories to non-fishing friends, ~~always~~ include a "fish-spotting" dog!

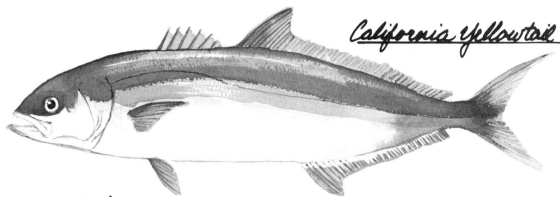

California Yellowtail

This beautiful, popular, good-eating fish is an Amberjack.
He has a bright yellow tail and a yellow stripe down his side, which I guess in the fish's world means that he's brave — for that's what he is!

Yellowtail (Seriola dorsalis)

He is usually referred to as the CALIFORNIA YELLOWTAIL, so as not to confuse him with a number of far lesser fish that are called by that name in various seas of the world (including a piddling Snapper in Florida). The California Yellowtail is certainly *one* of the, if not *the,* most popular gamefish on the southern West Coast.

He is actually an *Amberjack* and travels in rather large schools. He seems to migrate or move north up the coast from Baja in the spring to the waters off Southern California, where he is most commonly found off San Diego out around the Coronado Islands. In the fall he begins moving south toward Baja again. There is literally no trick at all to spotting the huge schools when they arrive in the Sea of Cortez. They seem to be everywhere, pushing along at the surface and making the water boil as they tear into the baitfish. At times you find your boat surrounded by great 20- to 30-pound fish. They will take cast or trolled lures without hesitation. I have found my favorite bucktails and Rapalas to be excellent. They are fine fish on the table. I suggest that you keep one for dinner so that you can build up your strength to go out and catch and release more.

Part Three
Tackle

What equipment you need for fishing with rod and reel breaks down into a number of different concepts in tackle. *No one "type"* is ideally suited to all manners of fishing: in truth, within the framework of even one type, application and intent vary so greatly that you might as well compare tricycles and eighteen-wheel logging trucks.

Spinning tackle, for example, varies all the way from the extreme ultra-light. The entire ultra-light outfit weighs just a few ounces and is designed for the pleasure of taking Trout in low and clear water on "cobwebs" (lines that test in strength from one to three pounds and can cast a very small lure that weighs next to nothing: 1/16th to 1/20th ounce). Now, contrast that with a spinning reel that by itself weighs close to two pounds and is mounted on a heavy-duty ten-foot surf rod that weighs another two pounds and handles a couple of hundred yards of thirty-pound test line. An outfit like that could easily handle a fish a hundred times the size of your day's biggest Trout.

So let's take a look at the types of gear: spinning, spincasting, baitcasting, surfcasting, trolling, and big game.

Spinning:

Spinning gear is, I am sure, the most popular type of gear in use today, of course with good reason. For one thing spinning is a technique that's easy to master. A novice can cast like an expert in almost no time at all. There is no such thing as a "backlash" with this type of tackle. The line comes "spinning" off a *fixed* spool; there is no inertia to overcome and little friction to worry about.

I was by no means the first fisherman in the country to use spinning gear, but I was certainly *one of the first*. Once again I got lucky when I was a kid. A gentleman by the name of Bache Brown lived in my town and was a close friend. Mr. Brown introduced spinning to America and to me. It was a method and design for fishing that he had discovered in France back in the thirties. "Spinning" had been in use in Europe for quite a few years. Why it took so long to reach America, I have absolutely no idea. But thanks to

Spinning Reel

This is a sketch of that little Avocet Micron that I told you I have owned for over 20 years. It certainly helps you take care of & love your's as much.

handle/crank

anti-reverse lock

cup or flyer

foot peg

bail

line spool

brake or drag lever

line roller

Spinning Rod

Rod for face housing

Spincast Reel

This sketch is of a light, freshwater model by Daiwa.

Thumb operated line release button.

star drag

Bait Casting Rod

For use with either a Cast or Bait Casting Reel.

This sketch is of my "Pflueger" supreme. I've had it a long time but it still works like a fine watch.

Bait Casting Reel

level wind guide

star drag star pre-spool button

brake & free spool lever

Fly Rod

Surf Casting or Bait Casting Reel my sketch shows a Penn #9 model.

star drag

extra wide spool

Fly Rod

Fly Reel

This is a sketch that I made of my favorite little Fly Reel. It is made by Hardy.

↑ _Surf Rod_ is a two handed affair. It also comes in spinning models.

harness strap

harness strap brackets

roller guides and tip to reduce friction.

Big Game fishing rod.

drag control lever

drag preset dial

reel clamp or forward brace

This is a sketch that I made of the beautiful Penn International.

Mr. Brown it crossed the ocean. He gave me one of his reels back in the late thirties, or perhaps in 1940. It was called Bache Brown Luxor, and when he gave it to me I'll admit I just stared with a polite frozen smile on my face. "Thank you," I said, knowing the while (antibacklash expert that I was) that here was something so funny and radical that it would never catch on or catch fish.

You might well recall my Florida boy attitude about flyrods when I was young. I put the outfit away, only to have my mind and my life changed the very next day when an old fisherman friend, who had also been given an outfit, stopped by with a string of Spotted Seatrout the likes of which I'd never seen before, except perhaps on one of the commercial trout-fishing boats. My eyes almost came out of their sockets. "The Bache Brown," he said, almost in a whisper, "the Bache Brown, we've got to keep this to ourselves!" I almost broke my neck getting rigged up and down to the bay. The following day found me spreading the word all over town, which I am happy to report was Mr. Brown's intent all along.

SPINNING: BREAKDOWN INTO TACKLE CLASSIFICATIONS
Ultra-light

This is my favorite all-around tackle for Trout except on the biggest and roughest of rivers. It is ideal for small-stream fishing and working the shores of a lake.

Ultra-light rods range from 4½ to 6½ feet in length and weigh 1⅝ to 3 ounces. The line should be 1- to 3-pound test. You should be able to handle lures that range from 1/16 to 1/4 oz.

There are a number of good ultra-light mini reels on the market. Most of the better manufacturers cater to the growing market for this gear. Just make sure that you buy the *very best* that you can afford, as ultra-light spinning requires top-rated equipment, particularly as regards the drag mechanism (there is no room to play around with an uneven brake when you go fishing with cobwebs). Although I do not like to assume the role of consumer advocate, I feel that I'd be remiss if I did not at least make a few suggestions about products that I have used with success. My favorite ultra-light reel of all time (and I'm not even sure that it's made any more) is an Alcedo Micron. I have owned mine for twenty-plus years. It is still going strong after thousands of fish and is as smooth as the day that I bought it. Another reel in this class that I like quite a lot is the Quick # 110. (Nothing manufactured today is in a class with my Micron, but this one seems to be a family favorite; all my kids use them . . . which means they can take a fair amount of abuse.)

Next in line, and one that I'm just getting into (I like it a lot), is the Daiwa SS No. 1, a small, attractive and sturdy reel.

Exceptional reels are made by the Orvis Co., Shakespeare, Garcia Mitchell, Ocean City, and Penn. Check with your dealer *and make sure that the reel that you buy* has a good name and good people behind it (*before* you get behind it).

Now as to rod manufacturers, there are more than you can shake a fiberglass stick at. But, it would definitely pay you to look into the Fenwick line, which includes a wide range of quality rods. Cortland is another great favorite rod-maker of mine. Cortland has an ultra-light model (# UL 2000) that is 5 feet long and weighs 2 ounces. It's a dandy. (If you get one for your Dad, you'll probably wind up using every excuse to borrow it.)

If you want to, and can afford to, step up in price but also in *quality*. Look at one of the newer *graphite* rods. (I wish I could afford to buy each of my kids one, not to mention one for *my* old tired wrist.) These graphites are beauties. Check out both Orvis and Fenwick (who started all this business with graphite).

Actually, my boys and I make most of our own rods and have done so for a long time. It's a great deal of fun and one way that a dedicated fisherman can afford to have a couple of dozen rods hanging about. A great deal of pride goes into custom-making your own, but I can tell you right now that the very next ultra-light rod I wear out I'm buying one that I looked at, made by Fenwick. Its 5½ feet long and weighs one ounce and a half. I might never stop fishing.

Light Tackle: Trout, Bass, and fun

Rods: 6½ to 7½ feet.
Weight: from 3 to 5⅝ ounces.
Line range: 4- to 8-pound test.

When you go for your reel, look at *general freshwater* reels. Let your dealer help you match up your equipment. I suggest that you deal with only the most reputable sporting goods dealers. You might look for the sign reading "Certified Pro Shop" in the window. This guy will know what you are talking about, and most likely he'll have what you need. Most of the shopping-center-type drugstores and places like that might be able to give you a pretty good price, but remember! they probably are better qualified to give you moon-landing instructions than fishing-tackle advice.

A good way for you to learn about tackle is to pick up the catalogs put out by the top manufacturers. Some are free; others mght cost a couple of quarters; but they are filled with good advice, and at least recommend "Balanced" equipment.

Medium Tackle:

Here we move up to bigger fishing conditions, heavier Trout, Bass, Pike and that group.

The rod is usually 6 to 7 feet long and weighs from about 4⅜ to 5⅞ ounces. Lines will test out at between 6 to 12 pounds. The reel will probably be designated "medium fresh" or "light saltwater." (Most manufacturers have their own individual way of describing their outfits and usually, and *certainly should*, recommend the range of fish that an outfit is designed for.)

Heavy Freshwater:

When you get to these outfits, you are talking about Salmon and Steelhead, large Muskies and Pike. You would or could use the same outfit for light or medium *saltwater* fishing. Your rod will be about 6 to 7 feet long and weigh in the neighborhood of 6 ounces. Line, 8- to 15-pound test (this is just about as heavy as I like to go—for anything).

As you can see, we have run out of freshwater and find ourselves in the *salt*. That light-to-*medium* saltwater outfit mentioned above is perhaps the happiest choice of all for most saltwater fishing. Certainly it's just about right for the Stripers and Blues as well as Bonefish and small Tarpon (15—30 pounds). Anything larger is pretty much a guess. I personally prefer to take my chances more on the light side than go for the very heavy stuff (which is nothing but tiring to use and gives very little help on truly big fish that don't care to be caught). For example, you and your Dad are out after "football"-sized Tuna (which, by far and away, most of them are). You'll have absolutely no trouble with a medium or light-heavy spinning outfit that is loaded with 250 yards of ten-to-fifteen-pound test line. In fact, as you know, you'll have a heck of a lot more fun.

Now comes along a really big Bluefin and he hits. Your chances of landing him are just as good as they would be if you were using a really big heavy-duty outfit or in fact an ultra-light little Trout outfit. In other words, it wouldn't make one bit of difference to a five-hundred-pound Tuna on his way to Novia Scotia what you were using in the way of spinning-type tackle. He'd simply take it away from you and show it off to his friends on vacation up north.

"Why, it's nothing," an extra large pal might observe. "I got a fisherman too when I picked *my* outfit up in the very same spot."

Spincasting:

The same principles apply to *spincasting* that applied to *spinning*. Both use fixed-spool-type reels from which the line spins off in coils. The difference is that the spincasting reel is a closed-face affair and is generally mounted on a *baitcasting* rod, which is a rod with an offset or decorbed handle. Its primary advantage, of course, over the older design of *baitcasting* reels in which the spool revolved and great expertise was demanded in the use of your thumb to control the common backlash, is in its fewer demands on the fisherman. Using the spincasting reel gives you a wonderful reel-and-rod combination for plug-casting for Bass. It requires practically no dexterity on the part of the fisherman at all. The line is controlled on the cast by your thumb, which has nothing more important to do than to press or to release a button. If you can turn on the hall lights, you are well on your way to being an expert with this outfit. The big disadvantage as far as I am concerned is that, because the line generates a degree of friction as it spins out of the housing, it is not suitable for the very light lures I most enjoy. They require very light line and no friction at all at least for casting a respectable distance.

Most of the outfits that are matched up for this type of spinning start in the medium-light and medium range. All I can add is that because of their trouble-free operation they are ideal for you and your Dad if you decide that you want to fish a lot in the dark for big "Lunker" Bass.

Most manufacturers put out a good line of these reels. Some of the leaders are Zebco, Garcia, Shakespeare, True Temper, Pflueger, Heddon, and Daiwa. There are, of course, many more, so I would suggest that you shop around, talk with your pro shop, and try a few out until you find the one designed with you in mind.

Baitcasting:

In many ways, this is my favorite form of fishing. I suppose that this has a great deal to do with the fact that this is where I started, whipping up all those Mackerel out on the bridge. But I think it's more than just that. Baitcasting reels have always been a watchmaker's craft. Because of the friction and inertia of the revolving spool reel, everything about them had to be more than just a little precise. I remember the ruby-red jewels on the pivot-end nuts, and the dream I had of someday owning a level-wind reel (which by the time I was eleven I certainly did, only to find that the pawl and the worm mechanism couldn't live up to the pressure of my "Mackerel whip" retrieve). I spent more time down in Tucker's, the local sporting goods store, getting my reel put into proper order than I did out on the bridge.

The first reel I owned with a level-wind mechanism was an Akron, manufactured by Pflueger. What a wonderful reel it was! I can still hear it whine as the line traveled out and to this day fall into a certain rhythm whenever I crank a baitcaster. There was and still is something of magic in baitcasting reels. If you can and do master the art, you will find that this is the most accurate of all casting methods. An expert can feather the spool with his thumb and just guide his lure right to the spot that he wants it to go. Despite all the talk of inertia and friction, a fisherman with really fine and balanced equipment can reach out to the envy of most spinning enthusiasts. Of course, you will be using heavier weights to overcome all the problems.

Again I caution: Buy only the best. Stick to "name" manufacturers. You can seldom go wrong with Pflueger or Shakespeare, and you'd have to go some really to find a much finer reel than those put out by Garcia; their Ambassadeur line is really top-notch. When you go to pick out a reel, spend some time. Get the feel and the balance when it's mounted on a rod that you want or will use. Look for the watchmaker's smoothness. That's what will pay off in the end.

As to rods, again the choice is all up to you: light, medium, or heavy.

The light would be a freshwater stick; the medium is sort of a cross-over and perhaps your best choice. Most rods in this range will go about 2½ to 3 ounces, line 8- to 15-pound test.

The heavy-duty is perhaps 5½ to 6 feet in length, with a shaft weight of 3 or more ounces; the line weight is 12 to 20 pounds test. Again, take a look at the range of rods made out of graphite. I'd suggest you pay some attention to the Fenwicks.

Another rod I suggest that you look at is called the Florida rod. As a rule, this is a rather long-handled affair, with a shaft of close to 6 or 6½ feet. Floridas are fairly stiff rods for whipping those bucktails, a medium rod that can easily handle a fairly big Tarpon. Most of the ones that I've owned were custom-made, but I'm sure you can find the equivalent made by one of the manufacturers I mentioned, all of whom have a very wide range of equipment.

Surf Casting:

Here we come to those big sticks that are designed to cast a heavy lure right into the teeth of a gale over high surf.

Surf outfits can be either spinning or revolving-spool reels. I suppose it all depends on what you prefer. Both types accomplish the trick rather nicely. I personally prefer the revolving spool for this type of fishing. It just seems to me to be slightly more rugged and less prone to problems.

The traditional surf stick is a rod that runs somewhere from 9½ to 12 feet in length and can weigh as much as a couple of pounds. The average weight would be closer to 22 or 24 ounces, which is still a pretty big handful (actually two handfuls, as these are two-handed rods). The reel is called a squidding reel and is a wide-spool construction. It should have both a *free* spool feature and a star drag. You will find that most surf fishermen use reels designed and manufactured by Penn. Most of the reels turned out of this type by other manufacturers are equally good. Take a look at Garcia or Ocean City before you go jumping into the waves.

The line I would prefer for the squidding reels would be braided nylon, 30 or 36 pounds test. Your reel should be able to carry between 200 and 250 yards of line.

The spinning outfits by their nature carry somewhat lighter weight line, usually in the 15- to 20-pound range. They will also handle somewhat smaller lures than the conventional rigs: 2 to 4 ounces of weight as compared to the 4 to 6 ounces that seem to be favored by the squidders.

I would suggest that you outfit yourself with at least hip boots (I prefer waders). Surfing can be a cold lonely sport. Most surf fishermen carry a shoulder-strap bag for their tackle and lures. It's a good idea to throw in a sandwich and rain gear. Also in that bag I would carry a good assortment of metal squid lures. They are wonderful producers when fished in the surf. Include a few bucktails too, for, as you know, they are, as usual, unusually good. At night, if there is any chance at all that Stripers or Blues might be about, I'd have a couple of surface-type poppers. A couple of favorites are the Point Jude pop along and the Atom spinatom.

Trolling:

Technically, anything you use to pull a lure or a bait behind a boat that is moving is "trolling equipment." Often, on some of the small mountain lakes that I love, when the fishing is slow from the shore I move out in my canoe and troll. I use the same little outfit that I did when I was wading and casting the shore. I paddle along, as much for the exercise and the fun as for the fish. I am trolling and therefore my outfit is a trolling outfit (technically).

But it is the same kind of "technically" as when you jump in the air and are "technically" flying. What a difficult "technical" way it would be for you to get from the Florida Keys to the Sea of Cortez flying like that!

There are all sorts of reels, rods, and lines that have been designed just for trolling. You *would not,* and in most cases *could not,* cast with them.

Freshwater trolling on the big lakes involves equipment that enables you to get down near the bottom for the big Lake Trout and, of course, others. Most people have no understanding of just how deep some of our lakes can be. For example, in the Great Lakes it is often necessary to go down to depths of 300 to 600 feet to catch Lake Trout. And, believe me, if you tried to reach those kinds of limits with ordinary old fishing line, you'd need at least a few thousand yards and a few pounds of weight (hardly a great fishing thrill). Fortunately for those who might like this kind of sport, special lines and reels have been manufactured. There are two types of lines in general use for deep trolling. One is *metal,* a line (usually) made of Monel (a nickel alloy); the other is lead core, which is regular line that's been woven around a thin thread of lead for the core. Both sink quickly and deeply without the addition of a great deal of lead weight added to your terminal tackle.

Wire line is somewhat tricky to use. It kinks rather easily and can backlash into one horrible mess. Special very narrow and deep-spooled reels are used to control it; usually these have free spool and star drag features. Remember, if you go in for this "sport," that it takes approximately 100 yards of line to reach a depth of 50 feet, so you must know the depth of the lake that you intend to fish; you might need 500 yards of wire (hopefully not as a rule). Lead core, except for its obvious weight, handles pretty much like any normal dacron-type line. Its diameter per pound of breaking test is far greater than wire's is. Therefore it is not as ideal for the truly great depths. If you're using wire, it's a good idea to have a rod with roller guides, or at least guides made of carboloy, as wire will cut most any other type.

Saltwater and Big Game:

This is the kind of trolling I like. In fact, it's really the name of the game. The capture of most *oceanic* wanderers is accomplished by trolling.

And here again we have very specialized equipment. In fact, I think you could say that it's "specialized formally."

Most saltwater outfits conform to standards as to weight of equipment and breaking-strength of the line. The standards are set by the I.G.F.A. (International Game Fish Association), a group that was founded in 1939 and has its headquarters in Fort Lauderdale, Florida. The Association keeps all the records of who caught what record fish and just where. Because of the number of records and the questions about *which* fish qualify for *what* classification, etc., it gets rather complicated or at least requires tables and charts to keep up with all of the facts. I shall therefore just talk about tackle and try to simplify it for you.

The classes of tackle would be
(decided by the breaking test of the line and the weight of the rod tip):

	LINE	ROD TIP	RECOMMENDED REEL
Very Light:	8 lb. test and up to 12	6 oz.	1/0—4/0
Light:	20 lb. test and up to 30	6—9 oz.	2/0—4/0
Medium:	30 lb. test and up to 50	9—12 oz.	6/0—9/0
Heavy:	50 lb. test and up to 80	16—24 oz.	10/0—12/0
Very Heavy:	80 lb. test and up to 130	24—30 oz.	14/0—16/0

Most of the time the class of tackle is referred to simply by the line weight. For example, when you speak of "light" tackle, you would say 20-pound class, and that is the way it is specified by the manufacturer right on your rod: #20. Just pick out a light-tackle reel, 2/0, 3/0, or 4/0, load it up with 20-pound test line, and everything should be in balance.

Terminal Gear

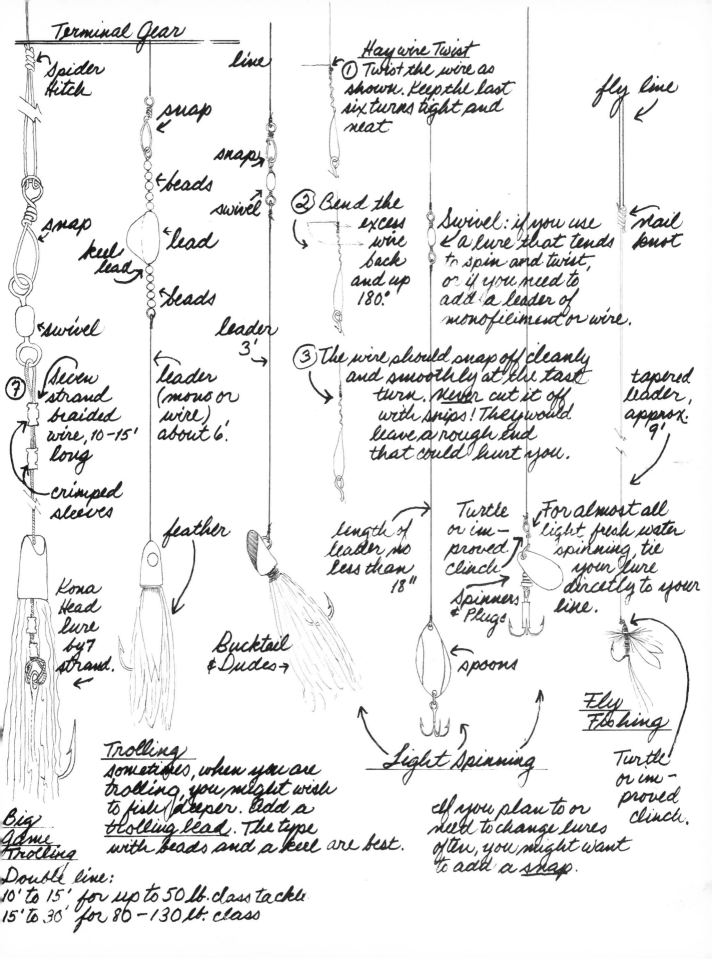

Spider Hitch

line

snap

snap

beads

swivel

lead

beads

leader 3'

snap

keel lead

lead

swivel

leader (mono or wire) about 6'

⑦ Seven strand braided wire, 10-15' long

crimped sleeves

Kona Head Lure by 7 strand.

feather

Bucktail & Dudes →

Hay wire Twist

① Twist the wire as shown. Keep the last six turns tight and neat

② Bend the excess wire back and up 180.°

③ The wire should snap off cleanly and smoothly at the last turn. Never cut it off with snips! They would leave a rough end that could hurt you.

length of leader no less than 18"

Swivel: if you use a lure that tends to spin and twist, or if you need to add a leader of monofilament or wire.

Turtle or improved clinch

Spinners & Plugs →

spoons

fly line

nail knot

tapered leader, approx. 9'

For almost all light fresh water spinning, tie your lure directly to your line.

Fly Fishing

Turtle or improved clinch.

Light Spinning

Trolling
sometimes, when you are trolling, you might wish to fish deeper. Add a trolling lead. The type with beads and a keel are best.

If you plan to or need to change lures often, you might want to add a snap.

Big Game Trolling

Double line:
10' to 15' for up to 50 lb. class tackle
15' to 30' for 80 - 130 lb. class

A few basic knots you should teach your dad.

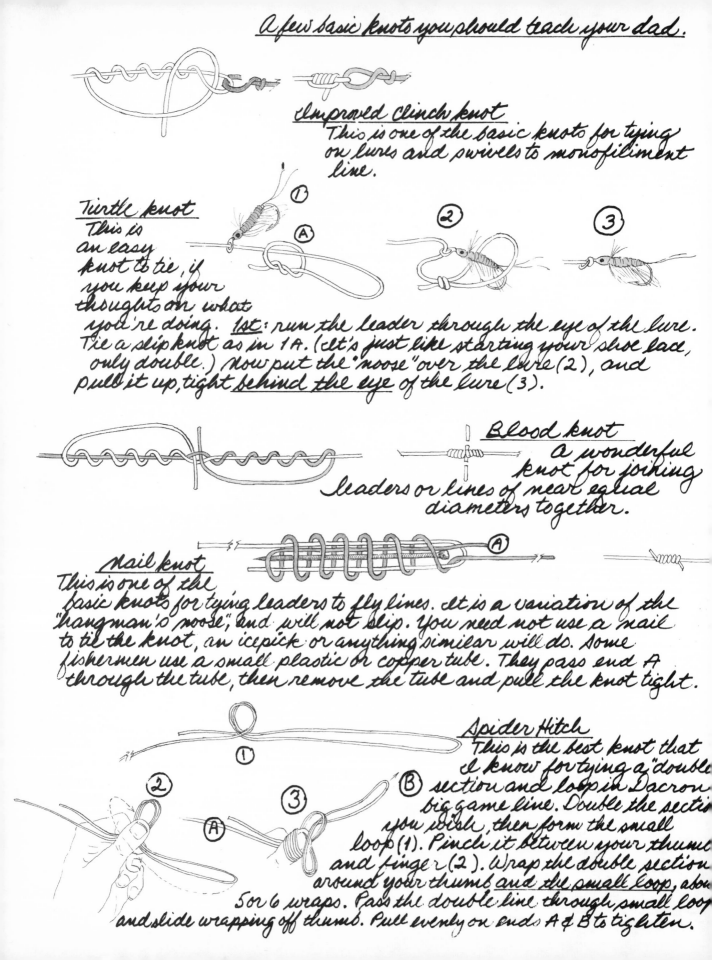

Improved Clinch Knot

This is one of the basic knots for tying on lures and swivels to monofiliment line.

Turtle Knot

This is an easy knot to tie, if you keep your thoughts on what you're doing. <u>1st:</u> run the leader through the eye of the lure. Tie a slip knot as in 1A. (It's just like starting your shoe lace, only double.) Now put the "noose" over the lure (2), and pull it up, tight <u>behind the eye</u> of the lure (3).

Blood Knot

A wonderful knot for joining leaders or lines of near equal diameters together.

Nail Knot

This is one of the basic knots for tying leaders to fly lines. It is a variation of the "hangman's noose", and will not slip. You need not use a nail to tie the knot, an icepick or anything similar will do. Some fishermen use a small plastic or copper tube. They pass end A through the tube, then remove the tube and pull the knot tight.

Spider Hitch

This is the best knot that I know for tying a "double" section and loop in Dacron big game line. Double the section you wish, then form the small loop (1). Pinch it between your thumb and finger (2). Wrap the double section around your thumb <u>and the small loop</u>, about 5 or 6 wraps. Pass the double line through small loop and slide wrapping off thumb. Pull evenly on ends A & B to tighten.

All big game species of fish, like the Billfish and Tunas, would certainly qualify for all classes of tackle. The *smaller game fish* would not. For example, take the wonderful Bonefish. He wouldn't be a wonderful fish at all if you caught him on 130-pound test line and a rod that weighed 30 ounces. As a matter of fact, a world's record Bonefish might be just about the right size to rig up for bait on an outfit like that.

I hope that you understand the point that I make. Your outfit is *balanced,* and in such a way by the I.G.F.A. as to be in balance also with the size and species of fish that your outfit is intended to take. That is not only fair to the fish, but it also gives you a good chance at a record *if* you fish *very light* or *light.*

Let me explain why and how it might work. Let's take the Bluefin Tuna. As you know, he gets very big. But the world's record for 12-lb. test line is (I believe) 56 pounds, which is not very big for a Tuna. But almost nobody goes fishing for Bluefins with 12-lb. test line. Your chances of hooking a world's record fish would be good. Getting him in would be up to you. (Just to give you some heart for the job, let me remind you that an Atlantic Blue Marlin was taken on a #12 outfit—and he weighed 448 pounds.)

Most big game fishing line is dacron, although many fishermen fish with and prefer monofilament.

Study the pictures of knot and terminal gear that I've drawn for you on pages 215 and 216. They will help keep your Dad all together.

Now, Dad might surprise you by mentioning the "old" method of rating the weight of approved big game tackle. Linen line, and particularly cuttyhunk, was the line that big-game fishermen used before modern and more durable lines came along back in the fifties. Each thread of the linen line was measured at three pounds of breaking strength. Very LIGHT TACKLE called for three threads of linen, which was, as you can figure, a line that tested at 9 lbs. The rod tip for this outfit would have been the same as that required today, 6 ounces. It was therefore referred to as 3/6 tackle. There was 6/9 tackle, for example, which would be 6 threads of linen (18 lb. test) and a 9-ounce rod tip. Under the standards, 72 thread was the largest made. It tested at 216 pounds. If, in fact, your Dad did know this old method of measuring line, don't be surprised if he sighs and says something like "I sure miss that cuttyhunk line . . . that old 39 thread was just about perfect."

And in case you don't know it, he's right.

In closing the book, I want you to know, little teacher, that I consider you (*Dadmorus teacherotus*) the finest catch of them all. I release you with love, as I have most of the fish, with the hope that you and your Dad will move out into the world of sparkling adventure.

Naturally, I urge, as they say, "Take care," and I mean of the fish as well as yourselves, so that someday when you have your own little alevin or parr he or she might be able to do it all over again.

Now let me suggest a few other books you might enjoy starting your fishing library with:

THE STREAM CONSERVATION HANDBOOK by Michael J. Migel
(with the hopes that it might get you involved)

THE LIFE STORY OF THE FISH: HIS MANNERS and MORALS, by Brian Curtis (to learn all about fish)

McLANE'S STANDARD FISHING ENCYCLOPEDIA by A. J. McLane
(the very finest and most complete book on all phases of fishing)

TROUT FISHING by Joe Brooks
(because it's one of the best and I loved him)

THE ATLANTIC SALMON by Lee Wulff
(there's nothing left to be said about *Salmo salar* or a better way to say it than this; it's a classic)

THE FISHING IN PRINT by Arnold Gingrich
(for anyone who loves reading and wants a marvelous tour through the history of angling literature)

Index

222

THIS BOOK WAS COMPOSED IN PALATINO
ON THE MERGENTHALER V-I-P
BY BEACON TYPESETTING, INC., PANORAMA CITY, CALIFORNIA
AND PRINTED AND BOUND BY R. R. DONNELLEY & SONS COMPANY,
CRAWFORDSVILLE, INDIANA.
BOOK DESIGN BY KADI KARIST TINT.